THE NEW JOURNALIST'S
GUIDE
TO FREELANCING

THE NEW JOURNALIST'S GUIDE

TO FREELANCING

*Building Your Career
in the New Media Landscape*

Meg Wilcox

broadview press

BROADVIEW PRESS— www.broadviewpress.com
Peterborough, Ontario, Canada

Founded in 1985, Broadview Press remains a wholly independent publishing house. Broadview's focus is on academic publishing; our titles are accessible to university and college students as well as scholars and general readers. With over 800 titles in print, Broadview has become a leading international publisher in the humanities, with world-wide distribution. Broadview is committed to environmentally responsible publishing and fair business practices.

Library and Archives Canada Cataloguing in Publication

Title: The new journalist's guide to freelancing : building your career in the new media landscape / Meg Wilcox.
Names: Wilcox, Meg, author.
Description: Includes bibliographical references and index.
Identifiers: Canadiana (print) 20220389233 | Canadiana (ebook) 20220389284 | ISBN 9781554815135 (softcover) | ISBN 9781770488649 (PDF) | ISBN 9781460408001 (EPUB)
Subjects: LCSH: Freelance journalism—Textbooks. | LCGFT: Textbooks.
Classification: LCC PN4784.F76 W55 2022 | DDC 808.06/607—dc23

Broadview Press handles its own distribution in North America:
PO Box 1243, Peterborough, Ontario K9J 7H5, Canada
555 Riverwalk Parkway, Tonawanda, NY 14150, USA
Tel: (705) 743-8990; Fax: (705) 743-8353
email: customerservice@broadviewpress.com

For all territories outside of North America, distribution is handled by Eurospan Group.

Broadview Press acknowledges the financial support of the Government of Canada for our publishing activities.

Edited by Tania Therien
Book design by Michel Vrana

PRINTED IN CANADA

For my students, past, present, and future—
I can't wait to see the great stories you'll tell.

Contents

Contents

Acknowledgments

First, the biggest of thank yous to the journalists who took the time to talk with me about their freelance experiences: Sonya Bell, Gabe Bergado, Desmond Cole, Rebecca Collard, Hilary Duff, Kat Eschner, Jennifer Kingsley, Jeremy Klaszus, Erin Lowry, Anupa Mistry, Coleman Molnar, Omar Mouallem, Waubgeshig Rice, Trevor Solway, and Roberta Staley. Your honesty and candor was so helpful in framing the concepts in this book, and I learned so much from our conversations.

A big thank you, as well, to those who helped connect me with sources, interviews, and information: Chris Berube, Jim Davies, Nana aba Duncan, Lauren Harper, Sean Holman, David Moscrop, Jen Norwell, Logan Peters, and Shama Rangwala.

I'd also like to thank the experts who took time to share their knowledge of the many facets of freelance:

- Mike Anderson at Inter Alia Law and Lagom Law for his expertise in media law and contracts, and Gabe Meister for his support on the American side of the law;
- Tova Epp at Artbooks, Jonathan Medows at CPA for Freelancers, and Liz Schieck at the New School of Finance for their tax insights;
- Vivian Le at 99% Invisible and Eli Lopez at the Washington Post for sharing their editor perspectives;
- And to Nasr Ahmed at CWA Canada, Nicole Cohen at the University of Toronto, Rafael Espinal at the Freelancers Union, and Don Genova with the Canadian Freelance Guild for their understanding of freelance work in the bigger labor picture.

I've been talking about writing this book in some way, shape, or form for the past 10 years, but it wouldn't have happened without the support of my friends, colleagues, and family. Many of the ideas in these chapters started while talking shop over pints at the pub, and it was those conversations that helped get them on the page. Whether you lent an ear, took a look at a rough draft, or gave me a place to stay as I worked on revisions—thank you! Special thanks to my sister, Cate Wilcox, for her design help and insight.

A million thanks (and Smudge Skittles) to Andrea Phillipson and the Mount Royal University Academic Writing Group for their support and keeping me on track with my writing, in spite of the many unexpected turns that came with a year of remote teaching. I'm also very appreciative of my brilliant colleagues at Mount Royal University Journalism and Broadcast Media Studies.

It is a pleasure and an honor to be able to live, work, and, most importantly, learn on Treaty 7 territory.

Thanks to the team at Broadview Press for helping me bring this book together, including Brett McLenithan, Marjorie Mather, and Tara Trueman, as well as Tania Therien for her keen eye with editing.

Finally, a special thanks to Anton deGroot for his constant support, whether in the form of a well-placed writing session snack or holding down the fort (and the menagerie) when I needed to get out of town to work. I appreciate your honest assessments on what unwieldy metaphors and less-than-funny jokes to cut—so, I'm sure, will the readers.

Introduction

It's a big day in a journalism student's life when they see their work in a real newspaper for the first time—for me, it was January 10, 2010. I had sold a class assignment to the Ottawa Citizen, a story about federal politicians and social media. What started as a draft for a features writing class was now on the front page of the Ottawa Citizen's Saturday Observer section. To see it all come together—the large-font headline, the sharp (color!) image, my first real byline—was such a thrill. I bought extra copies at the convenience store on my block to send back home.

After getting back to my apartment, I admired my name in the byline ... admittedly, I took my time with that. I was starting to get notifications from friends who were sharing the story on social media—another first! It was then that I realized, even though I'd signed a contract to be paid for the piece at 25 cents a word, I hadn't been paid for my work ... and, more importantly, I actually didn't know *how* to get paid. I emailed the city editor who had helped me with the story, and while I'm sure he wasn't expecting to give a crash course on invoicing that weekend, I'm still grateful he had the patience to do so.

It was a complete facepalm moment—but, looking back on it, it kind of makes sense. While I had a strong education in journalism itself, the practical points of freelancing were never addressed in my classes. Freelancing was always mentioned as an option to me and my classmates, but we never got into the nitty-gritty of how it actually worked. My professors' experiences in freelancing usually came after they had spent years at an established outlet and had made names for themselves, which was very different than when I set out as a new grad to start my career in journalism.

The job market in 2010 was ... difficult, to say the least. My summer internship at the Canadian Broadcasting Corporation (CBC) national newsroom wrapped up just as some significant job cuts were about to come down, and it was clear that the odds of finding a stable job there weren't in my favor. So, after my internship ended, I went to visit family in Austin. I was still applying to full-time media jobs, but wanted to learn about my options—and spent part of my downtime building my website and reading books on how to freelance. Most of the books I found were American, and while they helped me understand ways to run a freelance business, they left me with big gaps in understanding taxes and didn't address specific issues related to freelance journalism in Canada. Still, it was enough to get started, and I learned as I went along—each new pitch, each new gig, each new story helped me grow as a journalist and as a freelancer.

Over the past decade, I don't think anyone would claim the media industry has gotten any easier to navigate—as media grows and changes, so do the many options and opportunities for work. I have often complained that there isn't a comprehensive book on freelance journalism that includes the Canadian perspective and considers the issues new journalists might have getting started in freelance—this book is my attempt to help fill that gap, including specifics for journalists on both sides of the border. A lot of the advice in this book comes from my 10-plus years of experience as a freelance journalist, but it's also informed by the questions and conversations I have every day with my students as a journalism professor. And, because journalists never trust only one source, I spoke to about 30 other freelancers and freelance experts—from Vancouver to New York City to Beirut—to hear their stories and advice for journalists who are starting out. For me, these interviews highlighted that, while everyone experiences freelancing differently, we face many of the same challenges as we go about our work. I hope that, as you meet these freelancers throughout the book, you'll be inspired by the many ways you can use your journalism skills after graduation.

So what exactly is freelance journalism?

In its simplest form, to freelance means you work for yourself rather than for a company or organization full-time. And there isn't just one way to do it—talk to different freelancers and you'll see the field is as unique as they are. Some may have a steady day job, pitching stories and working on projects in their free time; others may rely solely on freelance work for their income. You can work short contracts with organizations, or come in as a temporary employee. As the world of work evolves, so does the definition of what it means to work freelance.

Being a freelancer isn't just a job title or classification—it's also a mindset. Freelancing means being engaged in your day-to-day work, coming up with pitches and ideas and projects you care about, and finding and developing networks that will pay you to make these projects a reality.

By this description, maybe freelancing doesn't sound like a great deal in terms of a career. It has its advantages and its disadvantages, and it's definitely not for everyone. That said, it's also a great way to create a flexible career that you get to build, or a way to get your foot in the door if you're looking for a more standard 9-to-5 media job.

Why this book?

Ten or 15 years ago, freelancing was one of many options for budding journalists. But now, as newsrooms are shrinking to fractions of their previous size, options for a traditional 9-to-5 job in the media have changed significantly. Today, you are more likely to work as a freelancer for the start of your career—maybe to develop your portfolio or demo reel, or to make connections at an established outlet. But freelancing isn't just a stepping stone to your next job—it's also a completely legitimate way to build your career as a journalist and could in fact be your end game.

Mixing your passion (journalism is your passion, right?!) and business can be tough—and there aren't any absolute best practices for how to go about it. We often hear about the importance of entrepreneurship, and while some of that advice can be helpful, there are many times where the work of a freelance journalist and the goals of a media start-up come into conflict, or don't apply at all.

This book doesn't hold all of the answers on how to build the perfect freelance career, if such a thing even exists. But it will introduce you to some of the concepts you'll want to be familiar with before you get started, and help guide you with questions and other things to consider as you start to make your way.

What kind of jobs can I get as a freelancer?

Many people might associate freelance journalism with writing for magazines, but there are lots of other types of freelance work out there. Think of any job in the field of journalism, and you can find a way to freelance it:

- writing for newspapers, both national and local
- writing for trade news and newsletters
- blogging and writing for online publications
- fact-checking and copyediting
- photography for print, magazine, or online
- producing radio, television, or film pieces for stations and networks
- video or podcast production
- creating social media content

... and so much more. You can freelance for news organizations, or you may choose to create content for non-news companies or clients.

In order not to get too bogged down in language specifics, you'll see that throughout the book I'll alternate using terms like "writing" or "producing" or "creating," as well as referring to "publications" or "media outlets" or "organizations." Most of the ideas we'll talk about apply to freelancing regardless of the medium you choose; when it's medium-specific, I'll let you know.

While you may feel like a beginner when it comes to the world of freelance, it's important to take a moment to acknowledge that your journalism training gives you a leg up over many other people looking to get into the field. You have a strong idea of what makes a good story, how to focus ideas, how to write clearly using proper formats, and how to consider an audience when producing your work. You *do* have skills that employers want and that will set you apart from others! Now, it's about marketing those skills.

So, what does it take to be a freelancer?

Seeing as anyone can give themselves the title of freelancer ... congrats, you already are one! In practice, successful freelancing is a mix of *being creative*—coming up with story ideas, creating your work—and *running a business*—selling yourself, selling your ideas, getting paid for your work.

In this book, we'll look at

- exploring different types of freelancing jobs: what they are, how they pay, and how you find them;
- building your brand as a journalist and how to find and connect with people to build your freelance network;
- pitching your story: where to pitch, what makes a great one, how to sell it ... and what happens after it gets accepted (or doesn't!);
- managing your freelance business: planning your finances, setting rates, getting paid, and how to plan for tax time;
- working within the law as a freelance journalist: from libel to copyright, and what to look for when negotiating a contract; and
- considering the bigger issues and challenges around freelance work, and how the gig economy fits into the bigger labor picture.

In many ways, freelancing is a less certain career path than a steady full-time job. There are a lot of issues—social, economic, and systemic—that are related to freelance journalism and working within the gig economy, which we'll talk about later in this book as well. But, with practice, knowing your value, and developing your network, you can build a freelance career and even make a good income. And if you're more interested in developing creative projects outside of a steady non-journalism job, freelancing can give you that outlet and some cash on the side.

To be a successful freelancer, you need to understand the many systems you'll be working within so you can make informed choices—whether that's where to pitch, what to charge, or how to file your taxes. My hope in writing this book is to introduce you to these systems so you can avoid some of the mistakes I made when starting out.

Ready? Onward!

Chapter 1:

What is freelance work?

In this chapter ...

- What types of freelance work are there, and how do they differ?
- How do you find freelance work?
- Is freelance work right for you?

In the media industry, freelance work comes in many shapes and forms. Some companies have specific terms they use for certain types of contract or freelance work, and many people use terms interchangeably, even if they aren't exactly the same thing.

For the purpose of this book, I define freelance as **any work that isn't a defined long-term job.** It's a broad definition, but it's important to be familiar with the many forms of work that comprise freelance life; you will likely take on a variety of jobs as you build your career. If you speak to a freelancer about their work, you'll likely hear that they balance multiple projects, each of which are contracted, supervised, and paid differently—so it helps to know the different types of work you may take on. Depending on the job, you will get paid in different ways. This matters because you will need to know how to actually *get* paid (e.g., Do you send an invoice? Do you fill a timesheet?) and what implications this may have for you come tax time. We'll talk more about financial planning and developing your business mindset in chapter 4.

To start, here's a brief overview of the types of freelance work you might encounter:

1. Paid by the piece

This is likely the most familiar type of freelance: when a journalist pitches and sells their work by the item. In this case, you reach out to a media outlet, network, or show and pitch your idea. If they like it, they'll get back to you and set the terms of the piece (focus, length, deadline, etc.). Pay is often determined by the word, or by the length of the final piece if you're working in broadcast. You then agree, deliver your work by the deadline, and work with the editor or producer until it's ready to publish.

As a freelancer, you supply your own gear to do your work, though some outlets might lend you extra recording gear or let you use a computer station to do editing if you don't have access and they have the space.

After your work is submitted and approved (or published) you invoice the agreed-upon amount for the work and you get paid! If you received an advance on your piece, you will bill for the remaining amount. Because you are not considered an employee, tax on your income is not deducted by the company, so you will have to set aside the taxes to be paid on that income yourself.

2. Temporary employment

Temporary employment, also known by many other names, like casual or backfill work, is generally used by media outlets to fill in their staffing gaps. You sign employment papers or an offer letter agreeing to the pay rate, and you will be scheduled or called in when you're needed for work. In this situation, employers may try to give you an estimate of how much work you'll get in a given week, but realistically there is no guaranteed amount of hours. Some weeks you may work a full-time equivalent; others not at all.

Many newsrooms will schedule their temporary staff about two weeks in advance, though those schedules can always change. You can also get same-day calls if an employee is sick and they need someone to fill in. While at work, you should be using company resources—computers, phones, recording, and editing gear.

With temporary work, you're classified as an employee, which means taxes are deducted from your wages, as well as any union dues or other work-related fees. You usually get paid by submitting a company timesheet with your hours and receive a paycheck on the same schedule as the rest of the company's employees.

While the name might suggest that this type of employment is tenuous (and it can be!), budget cuts in newsrooms have led to an increase in temporary staff work. You will meet people who have been "casuals" for years, some of whom work full-time or near full-time hours. There are also certain times of the year (like summer or winter holidays, when staff take vacation time) where work is more widely available for temporary employees.

Some outlets will put out postings when looking for temporary employees, but many won't. If there's a place you're interested in working for, it's worth reaching out to the hiring editor or producer to express your interest and share your resume and portfolio.

3. Contract employment

While most types of work involve signing a contract, contract work goes beyond signing a piece of paper. Contract employment is when you get hired by a company under specific terms and for a certain amount of time. The pay will be set based on the work outlined. Contracts can be for employee-type labor, like in a full-time newsroom where you come in, work as a regular reporter, and get paid by salary or by the hour. On the other hand, a contract could also determine the terms of work for a specific project, like editing a book, or an agreement to produce a certain number of print articles or radio pieces over a certain amount of time. In this case, the pay would usually be set out for the total project.

For the first example, you're likely considered an employee— you will use company gear and have taxes and other deductions taken from your income. For the second, you will likely be classified as a contractor, where you're considered self-employed. You will use your own gear, and no taxes will be deducted from your pay.

In any case, you will want to make sure you understand how you're being hired, the scope of the work, who is responsible for providing equipment, how you get paid, and when you get paid. There can be advantages to being considered both an employee or a contractor, as long as you know what to expect and can plan for it—mostly when working out your taxes. We'll discuss that more in chapter 6.

Contracts can add comfort or consistency to your work, but it's worth mentioning that contracts can be broken (sometimes with more notice than not—though that can apply to both sides!) So, while contract employment may feel a bit steadier than casual work, it doesn't mean the employer can't make changes along the way.

4. Mix and match

You aren't limited to just one type of freelance work—many journalists combine a mix of jobs to fill out their schedules and earn a living:

Kat Eschner, a freelance writer out of Toronto, currently serves as a contributing editor to Popular Science two days a week, which provides steady income while she pitches stories to publications across North America and Europe.

Erin Lowry, a financial writer based in New York City, has written three books, but also makes money from several other avenues: she writes finance articles for major American media outlets, produces financial literacy guides that she sells online, and does public speaking events.

Trevor Solway, a filmmaker in Alberta, balances making corporate videos with creating grant-funded documentaries and narrative films; he also founded and helps run the Napi Collective, a group of young Indigenous filmmakers from Siksika Nation.

You'll meet these journalists—and more!—as you continue through the book.

How do you find freelance work?

Just like the work itself, the field of freelance work is rather amorphous. You'll find a mix of traditional job-hunting methods and less-traditional techniques can land you freelance opportunities.

- Pitching stories to outlets is one of the best ways to start to network and land your first jobs. We'll walk through ways to decide which outlets to pitch to and how in chapters 2 and 3.

- Job boards and social media (particularly Twitter) can be a great place to find out what outlets are accepting pitches. If you're on the hunt for a longer term job, you can also check news outlet job boards for contract and permanent job opportunities.

- If you're interested in working as a temporary employee at a news outlet, reach out to the managing or hiring editor to see if there are opportunities available.

- Friends and family can also put you in touch with contacts looking to hire freelance or contract workers. Don't forget your circle of journalism school friends and your professors, who may have contacts to help you out.

- As you begin to build your freelance portfolio and grow your network, you will find that work will start to find you—companies are often on the hunt for good, reliable freelancers.

Is freelance work right for you?

If there was an easy answer to this question, this book would be a whole lot shorter!

There are many advantages to working freelance:

- It can help you build your portfolio and get your foot in the door at places you may want to work at full-time.

- It can give you the opportunity to get your work into major publications and outlets where working full-time might not be feasible.
- You can control many elements of your work—like the stories you pitch and where, your work hours (to some extent), and the coordination of freelancing with other jobs or responsibilities.
- If a 9-to-5 job at the office isn't for you, freelance is a way to keep things on the move—including running many pitches, projects, and ideas at once.
- It can be a great side job that allows you to use your skills to create and share stories, and can help provide additional income.

But that isn't to say there aren't a lot of challenges to freelancing, too:

- Pay rates for freelancers might feel good when you're starting out, but rates realistically haven't increased in 30 years.
- More and more outlets are requiring contracts that can restrict a freelancer's rights to their own work.
- Being able to control many elements of your work also means being responsible and self-motivated for your work, including regularly pitching new ideas to new people.
- As much as freelancing can give you some control over your work, you will still be limited by the requirements of your clients and your sources, and need to be flexible.
- Freelancing can involve a lot of time working alone.
- There is no such thing as a steady paycheck. Pay depends on the project and your client's payment schedule; what you earn monthly, let alone bi-weekly, will vary considerably, so it's important to plan for fluctuating income.

- Working as a freelancer can mean forgoing the plans and support that often come as an employee: health benefits, pensions, parental leave, and unemployment insurance. You can choose to contribute to private plans that exist where you live, but you will have to fund these benefits yourself.

Some of these pros and cons depend on who you are. Do you like working independently? Are you comfortable coming up with several new pitches every week and reaching out to sell your ideas? Are you up for planning around uneven monthly income?

Freelancing isn't for everyone, even though there are many ways in which you can navigate it—for example, you may find temporary work is your main source of income, and you can use your extra time to pitch stories to other outlets. You can take a part-time job to guarantee some income and plan to freelance around it ... and the freelance work may grow into a more full-time endeavor down the line. Or, all of this might sound horrible to you and you now want nothing to do with freelancing (if that's the case, maybe pass this book on to another kind soul who can use it).

The best answer I can give is that, as you read through the next chapters, take a moment every once in a while and ask yourself: Can I imagine myself doing these things? Does it appeal to me? Does it invigorate me? What worries me? What questions do I still have? Where can I go to get answers to these questions? This will help you develop a way to freelance that works for you—or help you recognize if it isn't a good fit. Ultimately, there is no right or wrong choice, just the choice that's right for you.

Anupa Mistry

writer and producer

Anupa Mistry started her post-secondary studies at the University of Toronto, where she earned an honors degree in political science in 2006.

"I vividly remember being in my last year of university and being like, 'What am I supposed to do after?' I had no idea," she says. "The only thing I could really think about was, since childhood, going back and getting a sense from teachers and report cards that I had good reading comprehension, that I was a good writer ... And I thought, 'Okay, maybe [this is] something that I could do.'"

Mistry entered Humber College's two-year journalism program thinking she would use her political science degree to become a political reporter—but she quickly found herself drawn to arts reporting. With the long-term goal of working at a major newspaper or magazine, she took her first full-time job working for Salon, a trade magazine for people working in the hair and beauty industry.

"It was fun, hanging out with hairstylists and interesting people ... You know, people who don't sit in front of a computer all day," she says. Over her two years at the magazine, Mistry enjoyed the events, openings, and free products. "They're just kind of immersed in a completely different world."

Mistry started as an editorial assistant and was then promoted to editorial roles. "[It was] a great experience in terms of learning how to put a magazine together, going through the whole editorial process, thinking about what it means to take your editorial calendar and then plan for a magazine and then think about translating that to digital."

But Mistry knew that, ultimately, she wanted to write about arts and culture. She started freelancing for Exclaim! and NOW Toronto on the side. When she left the magazine for a 9-to-5 marketing job, it gave her the space to pursue freelancing more aggressively on evenings and weekends. She built her portfolio and her name around Toronto, with articles in the Globe and Mail, Pitchfork, the Guardian, New York Magazine, FLARE, and more, and it led to contract work with the CBC. But she couldn't find a steady journalism job that felt like a good fit—until she was offered a staff job at The Fader in 2016 as they made a push into the Canadian market.

When The Fader closed their operations in Toronto, Mistry was disappointed. She had job offers, but all of them were from American outlets.

"The Fader was a dream job for me, you know? Getting to be there, getting to be at that job while also being like ... I could get my dream job in America, but no one in Canada would hire me!"

When one of her old bosses at The Fader offered Mistry a contract, she took it as sign to head to the US for a while and try something new.

"He was like, 'How about you come to New York? And you'll get paid to learn about video production.' And that was why I took the job at Vevo, because if I can learn a new skill, I think I should probably do that."

At Vevo, Mistry worked on their Original Content team and produced short-form documentaries and interviews with major labels and independent artists.

"I learned about how to start translating my storytelling skills to that medium. I learned what I like about video that I don't necessarily get from writing," she says. "And it also gave me the opportunity to take a break from writing.... Writing for the internet kind of broke me a little bit."

When Mistry lost her job at Vevo in a round of layoffs in 2018, she was ready to return to Toronto—and to freelance. This time, she wasn't taking the first job that came her way.

"It's been an important time for me to actually be able to figure out what the next iteration of my career is going to look like and do that a little bit more thoughtfully, instead of trying to fit myself into institutions or fit myself into roles like 'journalist' or 'TV writer,'" she says. "I can't go work for a big institution again ... having to write to the parameters and the expectations and the performance metrics and the sensibilities of everything that defines what it means to write on the internet."

As she navigates the next step in her career, Mistry is currently doing a mix of freelance work and developing film projects with her mentor's production company. It's a far cry from her start in magazines—and she credits the move with being open-minded and taking on opportunities as they come.

"I think it's important that, when opportunities come up, even if they don't seem like what you want to do, it's important to just consider them," she says. "When things didn't work, I pivoted and took risks and it's paid off—taking those risks has paid off big time just in terms of being able to open up into this world of production."

Chapter 2:

Building your brand ... and your network

In this chapter ...

- How to create and refine your online persona
- How to build your freelance network
- Informational interviews: how to request them and what to ask during them

Pretend you're an editor at a glossy, well-established magazine (let's dream big for a moment, shall we?). You've just read an email with a fantastic pitch—it's clear, focused, concise, and a great fit for your publication (don't worry, we're getting to how to do that in the next chapter).

Looking at the signature, the name of the journalist is unfamiliar to you. What would you do next? Probably do an online search, right? That's why it's so important as a freelancer to have a strong online presence that makes a great case for you and your work as a journalist. While it might feel a bit that you're putting the cart before the horse by focusing on your branding and promotion, you need a professional online presence to sell yourself as a journalist. Plus, taking the time to assess your work, determine your brand, and hone in on your future goals will help you see yourself as a professional and lay the groundwork for when you start to pitch producers and editors.

Your online persona

At a minimum, you'll want to have a simple website, a professional email address (don't worry, your NewDirection4eva@yahoo.com account can still be for personal use!) and a LinkedIn account. But, depending on where you want to specialize as a freelancer, you may want to consider Twitter, Facebook, Instagram, Medium, or others from the vast landscape of social media and publishing platforms. However, being on all social media platforms and not keeping them curated or updated is worse than being on a few and doing them well—so resist the urge to do it all at once and instead pick the options where you can see a direct benefit. You can always add accounts later if needed.

Website: a website is a necessity as it's your chance to showcase your work beyond the limited scope of a pitch. Your site doesn't have to be complicated—it can be as simple as having a photo, a short bio, and links to your work. It can also be a great place to house other creative content that can set you apart from the rest—like that great blog you write about where to find the best tacos in your hometown. Wherever you host your site, a short and simple URL or domain name adds a professional touch.

Email: a place where you can be contacted with a username that doesn't tip off your future employer to your favorite sport or band from high school. On that note, you may want to consider updating your voicemail message if you plan on using your personal phone for freelance work. Depending on where you host your website, you may also get free email accounts that you can set up.

LinkedIn: while certain fields of work use LinkedIn more than others, it's a simple way to create a mini-resume and professional-looking page that will rank high in online searches. Worth your time and the occasional update!

Nine tips to consider as you build your online presence:

1. Make sure your photo is recent, professional, and reflects the type of work you'd like to do. A picture

of you sitting in a Lamborghini makes sense if you want to write luxury car reviews, but less so if you're looking to do investigative or political reporting.

2. Whatever title you choose to give yourself, keep it consistent across platforms. You want people to find you easily and know it's you, whether they're on your website or LinkedIn.

3. You are selling yourself as a communicator—make sure your writing reflects that. Write in your voice and the best version of it—aim to be clear, concise, and error-free.

4. The goal of your website is for people to be able to reach you—so share a way to get in touch that isn't just a form submission. While it's understandable to not want to give out your cell number, it's helpful to at least include an email or social media account you check regularly.

5. Showcase only your best work, ideally pieces that relate to the work you're hoping to get as a freelancer. Update your portfolio as you get new jobs and opportunities, and don't feel obligated to keep old work on your website or portfolio as you create new and better pieces. Your work will change and grow from the portfolio you developed in school, and that's a good thing!

6. You may choose to create social media accounts specifically for work, but keep in mind that it becomes more accounts for you to manage and update. You may prefer to link your personal accounts instead—though remember that they will end up on your professional pages, so you may want to curate your personal updates appropriately.

7. Just because your online persona is professional doesn't mean it can't be fun! Your interests, quirks,

and hobbies are what make you unique and set you apart from other journalists—so don't shy away from sharing some of your personality. Editors are people, too, and they want to work with people who engage in the world around them and share similar values. You never know when your love of scuba might help clinch a writing job with an editor who's a fellow master diver.

8. Unless you're looking to sell web-design skills, keeping your site simple and easy to update means you are far more likely to actually update it. By adding embedded widgets or sections that pull from your latest Twitter or Instagram accounts, your website can feel fresh and regularly updated even if you haven't touched it in a while.

9. Have a few friends or people you trust take a look at your site and accounts to point out any issues with functionality, layout, typos, etc. Better for them to find than a future employer!

Once you have your online persona built, it's time to start ...

Building your network

Of course, before you can pitch somewhere, you need to know where to pitch. You need to begin developing your freelance network. This is probably the most intimidating part of free-lancing—finding who to reach out to and how. But, with a bit of practice, it will become second nature. Don't believe me? Think about how you felt before your first cold-call, your first interview, your first story—all things that you are now likely quite comfortable doing. Building your network uses all of the same skills, but this time with editors and other journalists instead of sources.

To find out who to pitch to, you'll need to pull out your journalist research skills and do a bit of digging.

Questions to ask as you begin to look for places to pitch

1. What types of work do you want to do?
2. What publications or outlets publish the work you want to do?
3. Which of these places accept freelance pitches?
4. Who is the main contact for freelance pitches?

The first question involves looking inward. Do you want to write features? Make radio documentaries? Create videos for social media? Are there certain beats or topics you'd like to focus on—like parenting, or politics, or the environment? You might have lots of interests that seem at odds with each other—that's OK! Write down the formats and the topics and ideas that spark your interest. Being able to pitch broadly is a good thing as a freelancer, and you can always narrow things down later if you feel you've cast your net too wide.

Now that you have a list of the types of freelance work you'd like to pitch—it's time to find places that publish the work you want to make. Start by listing the publications, shows, networks, websites that you admire that fit the bill, and then start the search for others that you haven't yet discovered. There are lots of online communities, podcasts, and social media accounts for freelancers full of great tips and tricks about outlets accepting freelance work, some of which you will find in chapter 3.

Online is a great place to start, but don't discount your real-life network: talk to friends, family, your professors, and other journalists and freelancers. Ask them about the best freelancing options they know about in your city, region, province, and beyond ... you may be surprised at what they come up with! Keep an eye out for places that are identified as freelancer-friendly: ones that pay well, pay on time, and treat their writers well. Take note of publications that don't pay or are known for not paying on time; you'll want to avoid those ones.

Once you have your list of places to pitch, you'll want to find out if they accept freelance pitches. Many websites will share this information, as well as a contact person (often in the "about" and "contact" sections at the bottom of the page). If it's unclear, you can always reach out to the organization, even just by calling the general number, to find out if they accept pitches and where to send them. When you can, avoid sending emails to general mailboxes, like info@magazine.com—try to get the names of editors and specific email accounts so you can reach someone directly.

By this point, you should be gathering a good-sized list of places to pitch and people to contact. I recommend gathering it all in one place, ideally in a spreadsheet, so it's easy to reference and update as you go.

Now that you have a list of places that accept the type of work you want to pitch, pick three that you would like to learn more about. Maybe you'll choose one big national outlet—something you'd like to work toward pitching to—as well as a couple of local publications that you know you have a better chance of working for. Maybe you'll pick three different types of companies, like a magazine, a website, and a radio station. Maybe you'll pick three at random. Your choice!

These will be your first informational interviews.

Informational interviews: The key to your next gig

You've probably done all sorts of interviews throughout your journalism degree, but the informational interview might be new to you—and it's a great tool as you begin to navigate the world of freelancing. Simply put, an informational interview is meeting up with someone (usually a potential employer) for an informal chat about who they are, the work they do, and any other questions you might have about work opportunities. Just because the meeting is often informal, don't confuse it with being unimportant. This is the opportunity to sell yourself and your ideas, and make a great impression before even sending in your first pitch—you will want to prepare and make it count.

Why are informational interviews important? Think back to being an editor at that glossy magazine earlier in the chapter and getting that great email pitch. Imagine, this time, that when you saw the name, you recognized it—because you had had a quick coffee and chat with the journalist last month. You're more likely to consider the pitch now, aren't you?

Informational interviews are a great way to get your foot in the door, show what you can do—and make sure that your name is familiar when your pitch lands in an editor's inbox. It's also a chance for you to suss out a publication and see if it's a place you actually want to pitch to or work for.

How to request an informational interview

You might be thinking, "There's no way a busy editor will make time for coffee/a phone chat with me!" But, from my experience, editors are willing, more likely than not, to make the time. Here's why:

1. Very few people actually reach out for informational interviews.
2. Any outlet that relies on freelancers needs to keep a number of great journalists in their arsenal, which means always keeping an eye out for new talent.

A quick phone call or email is all it takes to request an informational interview, and you might be surprised at how many people you hear back from. You now have a spreadsheet full of contacts—time to start reaching out!

As with any email correspondence, you want to keep things clear, concise, and professional. An email could be as simple as:

To: majoreditor@dreampublication.com
From: youremail@yourwebsite.com
Subject: Informational interview re: freelancing with your magazine

Ⓐ Dear Ms. Major Editor,

Hello! **Ⓑ** I'm a freelance journalist and recent grad from Mount Royal University's journalism program. My work has appeared in the Calgary Journal, and **Ⓒ** you can find my portfolio at mywebsite.com.

Ⓓ I'm a big fan of your album reviews and have some ideas for bands that would be a great fit for the section. **Ⓔ** I was wondering if you might have a bit of time to chat next week about freelance opportunities with your publication?

Ⓕ Thanks, and I look forward to hearing from you,
Future Freelancer
Ⓖ Cell: 403-123-4567
Yourwebsite.com
Any other social media accounts

Ⓐ Whenever you can, send emails directly to specific individuals, not generic email accounts, and be sure to address your email to their proper name so they know it's meant for them.

Ⓑ A brief line or two explaining who you are and some of the work you've done helps show the editor you have experience and are worth talking to. Even if it's your student publication, include it!

Ⓒ Don't bog down an email with attachments or long resumes—a web address will point them in the right direction if they need more information.

D Explain what interests you about the publication, without getting too long-winded. It helps the editor see that you know and care about the work they do.

E Make a clear ask for a time to meet. Options are coffee, phone, video chat ... or you can leave it more general and see what the editor suggests in their reply.

F It never hurts to be friendly and polite!

G Be sure that your email signature includes clearly marked ways of getting in touch with you, particularly by phone.

The best emails are short, but it's good to infuse a bit of personality—after all, this is an editor's first encounter with you and your writing. If you have any additional relevant information—like connections with the publication or one of its employees—be sure to include it (without making it too long!). A possible example:

To: majoreditor@dreampublication.com
From: youremail@yourwebsite.com
Subject: Informational interview re: freelancing with your magazine

A Dear Ms. Major Editor,

Hello! **B** I'm a freelance journalist and recent grad from Mount Royal University's journalism program. My work has appeared in the Calgary Journal, the Calgary Herald, and BeatRoute Magazine—you can find my portfolio at mywebsite.com.

C Jana Journalist, a colleague and classmate of mine, said that you may be looking to bring some new freelancers into the fold.

D I was wondering if you might have a bit of time to chat next week about freelance opportunities with your publication?

E Thanks, and I look forward to hearing from you. If you're not the best person to chat with, please feel free to forward this along to whoever is!

Best,
Future Freelancer
F Cell: 403-123-4567
Yourwebsite.com
Any other social media accounts

A Again, whenever you can, send emails that clearly state the recipient's name directly to specific individuals, not to generic email accounts.

B A brief line or two explaining who you are and some of the work you've done helps show the editor you have experience and are worth talking to. Your best publications should be listed here.

C If someone referred you to the job—especially someone who may already be freelancing with the publication or knows the editors—be sure to include it. Referral and word of mouth is a valuable currency in the world of freelance.

D Again, make a clear ask for a time to meet, so it's harder to ignore.

E You want to be clear and concise, but it never hurts to be personable! Asking them to forward on an email if they're the wrong person will hopefully mean your message will land on the right desk.

G Again, an email signature should include clearly marked ways of getting in touch with you, particularly by phone.

As you may have guessed, these are emails that will likely take some time to craft to get the voice and length right. Take the time to make a good first impression—and once you have a system that works, it will be simple to adjust depending on who you're reaching out to.

If you choose to call your contact instead, you will want to include the basics in any voicemail as well as a phone number where you can be reached. It also doesn't hurt to send a follow-up email in case it's your editor's preferred method of communication— just mention in your email that it's a follow-up to your voicemail.

What if I don't get a reply?

As you've no doubt learned from your work in journalism, it's OK to follow up! People are busy and email can fall to the wayside. If you haven't heard back in a week, feel free to send an email. You can also try writing to another editor at the same publication and see if you have better luck there. It's important to remember that silence isn't necessarily a rejection—sometimes, editors aren't looking for freelancers. Make a note to follow up again in a month or so—and even monthly, if it's a place you'd really like to work—when timing might be better, or when the editor admires your tenacity and finally writes you back.

What if I do get a reply?

Congratulations! Now that you have a meeting set, it's time to do some preparation. Here are some things to have ready for your informational interview:

1. Read up on the show or publication—know the latest episode or issue and what's in it.
2. Look up any other information about the company, like its owners and relevant sister publications.

3. Read up on the editor you're meeting—what are they responsible for? Is there a biography or information online on their career and experience? Be sure to take note of any highlights or things that interest you that you may want to ask about.
4. Draft up a list of questions to ask.
5. Prepare at least one, ideally a few, solid story pitches aimed at the publication and its audience. Be prepared to think on the fly if an editor has a story idea or two and asks you how you would go about chasing and producing the piece.

The first three steps rely on your research skills as a journalist: learn the product and learn the people in order to ask smart questions at your meeting. If you were an editor meeting with a journalist and they knew very little about your publication, would you want to hire them? Probably not. So be in the know!

In terms of developing questions for the interview, you want to learn both about the publication and how they go about working with their freelancers, which can look different at different outlets. You'll want to prepare questions that address both topics.

Questions to ask at your informational interview

1. What is your organization's pitching process?
2. What kinds of stories do you accept pitches for?
3. Are there certain formats you prefer?
4. What is your freelance rate?
5. How and when do you pay?
6. Are there certain times of the month or the year that are better to pitch?

By the end of your interview, you should know how this publication accepts pitches, what they're looking for, how much you would get paid and when. If you feel uncomfortable asking about money, practice it ahead of time and get used to talking about it. You're a professional journalist, and just because you're passionate about the work you do doesn't mean your work doesn't deserve to be compensated.... Plus, as we'll discuss in the next chapter, these are questions that editors expect and should be very comfortable discussing.

Aside from these questions, and any others you may have prepared, you will also want to have at least a couple of strong story pitches ready to go. While it might seem a bit like jumping the gun—isn't this just an informational interview?—pitches are the currency of freelancing, and having some good ones at a first meeting will put you on the editor's radar. It's also a chance to get some in-person feedback to find out if your ideas are on the right track, and for the editor to see how you approach storytelling. Plus, if one of your pitches is particularly good, you might even leave your informational interview with an assignment.

And that's it—the start of your freelance network!

For every informational interview you have, be sure to send a quick thank-you email to the editor you spoke with. Keep track in your spreadsheet who you've met, and update their contact information if necessary. Interview by interview, email by email, assignment by assignment, your spreadsheet and your network will slowly and surely start to grow.

Now, you're looking smart and professional online, and you've talked to at least a few places that know your name and might even take a look at your pitches. It's time to craft something great to send them, and that's our next chapter.

Gabe Bergado

editor and writer

When Gabe Bergado graduated from Northwestern University with a journalism degree in 2014, he wasn't entirely sure what he wanted to pursue as a job—but he knew that he didn't want to be an editorial assistant.

"When you're in a journalism program like Northwestern, or any really traditional one, it's the typical trajectory as you graduate. You become an editorial assistant or a junior reporter and you kind of work your way up," he explains.

With an interest in entertainment and culture reporting, Bergado was well suited to write on the boom of internet-culture stories that began making their way into media coverage. His internship at Mashable showed him there were other places— often at less traditional media outlets—where he could jump into writing and reporting right away as a staff writer.

"When I was graduating, I wasn't necessarily looking to apply at places like Hearst or Condé Nast, in all honesty."

After graduation, Bergado stayed in Evanston and waited for the right job to make his move to New York City—a fellowship writing for Mic.com. When the fellowship ended, he began freelancing for the Daily Dot, but they could only provide 20 hours a week—so he took a part-time internship with The Daily Beast.

"I think some people would be a little like, 'Oh, going back to being an intern or a fellow, that's a weird move.' And, in some ways, sure," he says. "But, to me, it's a good byline. It's a good place to be. I need the money. It's part-time. If full-time work comes along, there'd be no problem [leaving]."

His internship at The Daily Beast gave him a chance to interview his favorite stars (including a first interview with Carly Rae Jepsen) and to develop his entertainment writing, while the Daily Dot allowed Bergado to hone his reporting on "weird Internet stuff." Ultimately, the Daily Dot offered him more stable work.

In 2016, Bergado heard about a staff job with the site Inverse through a colleague—a way to gain editing experience and enjoy a steady salary. While it was a great learning experience, six months in Bergado heard his dream job had opened up at Teen Vogue—working with a fellow Northwestern journalism connection.

He credits the connection for helping get him an interview, but it's not the only factor.

"Obviously networks are important, but I think at the end of the day, your work has to stand for itself. And she wanted to hire me because she knew that I had an encyclopedic knowledge of every Disney channel original movie and was excited for Riverdale," he says.

It's one of the many ways his network of friends and colleagues has connected him to great writing opportunities.

"One of the best pieces of advice that I got in college from a professor is you're not there to impress your professors, you're there to impress each other," he says. "Of course, yes, you're impressing your boss, but the people who are at the same level as you when you're a student or a new intern, these are the people who are going to be looking out for you for the rest of your career in the industry, you know?"

Bergado lost his job at Teen Vogue in a large round of cuts at Condé Nast in May 2020 and is back to freelancing—with a portfolio, that includes articles in GQ, Nylon, Bon Appétit, Bazaar, Vogue, Wall Street Journal Magazine, and more. Though his roots are as a "start-up kid" and he wants to continue writing his brand of internet stories, his goals include getting published in Paper, the New York Times, and Rolling Stone.

"Those are obviously legacy publishers and I think it's really easy to get caught up in the name of what you're writing for," says Bergado. "[But] once you have [stories in] more concrete, bigger publications, you're able to charge more, which is just unfortunately kind of how it is. And if I'm going to have to play that game, I'm going to play the game."

Chapter 3:

Ready, set, pitch!

In this chapter ...

- Developing your pitch ideas
- The art of the pre-interview, and how to request one
- Writing, formatting, and submitting your pitch
- Ask a journalist: editors tell you what they look for in a great pitch
- How to follow up (without it being awkward!)
- Time is money: pitching and working efficiently
- Developing relationships with clients while setting boundaries for your work

Coming up with good story ideas consistently is one of the trickiest parts of being a journalist—but like most things, the more you work at it, the easier it will become. All good stories start with a question. It can be as simple as "what is happening?" to "why is this important?" ... with a plethora of possibilities in between. The key to generating good story ideas is to recognize the questions you have about the world around you—and then look at how you can answer these questions through your reporting.

The first step, regardless of what medium you want to free-lance in, is to keep up on the news of the day in general, as well as in the beats and publications or outlets that interest you. This will allow you to

- Put your pitches within a larger context—explain why your story matters

- Identify gaps in coverage that you can fill with your pitches
- Pitch local follows or angles to bigger stories (or vice versa!)

As for where to find story ideas ... as you likely know from experience, the opportunities are endless. You probably prefer to start on the internet—and it's a good place to start—because you can find lots of ideas from articles (news or otherwise) and social media posts and groups. But, beyond the easier finds, don't overlook other tried-and-true ways to find stories.

1. Hit the streets

The best way to report on the world around you is to get out there and talk to people in it! Conversations with people from all walks of life can lead to story ideas, even if it's as simple as a chat with the barista as you grab your coffee. Don't be afraid to ask questions that come to mind—the answers may surprise you.

It's not just people that can inspire ideas—using your skills of observation can also lead to questions that would make for a good story. Walking into the hospital the morning after a snowstorm, you help someone using a walker climb the snowy stairs to access admitting. Wait a minute—why are these spaces, designed to be accessible, not kept clear for those who need them? How does this affect the individuals using hospital resources throughout the winter? What are the solutions? Track down the answers to some of those questions, and you may just have a pitch on your hands.

Don't forget to check public notice boards for show posters, information on local events, even companies that are hiring. Anything that strikes you as new or unusual, and gets your attention, may be worth a bit of online searching to see if there's a story behind it.

2. Personal experience and curiosity

While your personal experience isn't enough to base an entire pitch or a story upon, questions you have about the world around you can be a start of a story idea. If you're wondering about something, you likely aren't the only one. Follow your curiosities—as long as you can show, through research, that they are in fact newsworthy and haven't been widely reported.

Don't forget your network of friends, family, colleagues, and acquaintances. Perhaps, while speaking to a friend, they tell you how they recently joined a recreational basketball league made up entirely of Sailor Moon fans—and they play exclusively in cosplay. Why not find out who runs the league and how long it has been running? If it's quite recent—or has a large following—or has had little to no coverage—it just might be a story worth pursuing.

Of course, not all questions we come up with are inherently newsworthy. As you've no doubt covered in class, there are many discussions around and definitions of news values that may help you decide if a question has journalistic value. Not all stories need to meet all of the traditional news values to be worth pursuing—but you will want to make sure they are present in some way, shape, or form in your story idea.

3. Documents

Going through documents can be a lot of work, but it's a great way to discover news that has gone unreported. Most governments, companies, and organizations now make documents available online, and this can lead you to endless amounts of information: annual and quarterly reports, newsletters, meeting minutes and agendas, statistics, and more. The key here is to look beyond the press releases that are widely distributed and likely already covered. Look for the unusual—have policies, fees, or agreements changed? Are numbers up? Down? Who might these changes affect—and why might that be important? Answer those questions and you will be well on your way to a story idea.

Freedom of information requests are another way to gain access to government documents. In Canada, you may hear them called freedom of information and privacy (FOIP) or access to information and privacy (ATIP) requests, and in the United States they're called freedom of information act (FOIA) requests.

While they're a great source of information, they do have their challenges:

1. While the paperwork isn't necessarily difficult to fill out, investigative reporters will tell you that there's an art to filling out these requests to actually get the answers you're looking for. It will take time, effort, and likely a few tries to start getting the information you need.

2. Each level of government is responsible for its own freedom of information legislation, which means that request systems, fees, and procedures will vary depending on whether you submit to the federal, state/provincial, or municipal government. It means being familiar with multiple systems, and knowing the jurisdiction that is responsible for your question.

3. In Canada, requests may cost money to submit. While some fees aren't much—i.e., for federal requests in Canada, the fee is $5—it can and will add up if you submit many requests. Other jurisdictions can cost more—like the City of Calgary, which charges $25 for each request. Governments may also charge an additional copying or processing fee to send you the information (some requests can generate thousands of pages of information!). In the United States, you typically won't have to pay anything to submit your request, but you will be quoted the processing fees and will need to decide if you want to pay for the information. As a freelancer, these are costs you will pay upfront before having stories to pitch. There are ways to appeal or reduce the fees, and there are even some organizations that will help you through the process, but it requires a lot of research and learning how to work within a complicated system—one that many journalists would say is purposefully complicated in order to deter requests.

4. Requests take some time for a reply. The general guideline for replies in Canada is 30 days and 20 in the United States, but departments have the ability to extend that deadline if they need more time to fulfill it. Speak to any journalist who fills many information requests for their work, and you will hear about some requests that take months—if not longer!—for a response.

For more information on the US federal freedom of information laws, the National Security Archive (http://nsarchive.gwu.edu/) has a comprehensive section on FOIA and how and where to submit requests. The FOIA wiki (http://foia.wiki) is created and maintained by a group of organizations promoting access to information, and the Reporters Committee for Freedom of the Press has an Open Government Guide (http://www.rcfp.org/open-government-guide/) that collects and maintains information around state freedom of information laws. In Canada, a good guide to start your research is *Your Right to Know: How to Use the Law to Get Government Secrets*, by Jim Bronskill and David McKie (2014).

A topic is not a story: Developing your idea

"I want to write a story about how the city's new transit construction is affecting residents in the northeast."

"I want to explain how fentanyl is affecting this rural community."

"There are hundreds of students protesting outside City Hall every week, and I want to find out why."

What do these three statements have in common? They're all topics or questions, not stories or pitches.

It's quite common for new journalists to pitch a topic rather than a story. And, to be honest, most great pitches start out as topics—so it's not a bad place to begin. But put yourself in the shoes of an editor and re-read those three ideas again: if you're responsible for bringing a show to air or a magazine to print, is that enough information for you to know if this is a newsworthy story that fits your needs? Probably not.

To pitch a proper story, you need to move beyond that initial question and start digging into the answer—and begin talking to the people who are involved in the story. Let's reimagine those topics as story pitches:

"According to a recent Angus Reid poll, 75 per cent of transit riders in the northeast are experiencing delays in their morning commute due to the city's new transit construction. One rider, Joni Angele, is one of hundreds of daily commuters who says her commute has nearly doubled in time. This story will follow Angele's transit experience, along with other northeast riders, to find out what it's like for those experiencing these delays—and will ask city transit officials why this is happening and when it will be fixed."

"Since attending a community workshop last year on how to use a Naloxone kit, nursing student Renee Lavoie has administered the drug to complete strangers four times—and saved their lives. This piece will profile Lavoie, the lives she's saved from drug overdose, and how it's changed her future career plans."

"Every Thursday afternoon, hundreds of high school students can be found protesting outside of City Hall—calling on the city to roll back massive cuts made to the Board of Education's budget. Despite missing an afternoon of school a week, Jordan Knox and the other protest organizers say it's a small price to pay to guarantee the quality of their education. This story will look at the cuts, the students who protest, and how school administrators are responding to the protests and the class absences."

As you can see from above, a solid pitch should include

1. Some background research and context;
2. A character or two—and highlight the other voices that will round out the piece; and
3. An idea as to where the story is likely going—what questions are you planning to answer, and who will answer them?

Certain types of stories—like covering an upcoming event—may be tougher to focus or pitch in this way. But working out some options for the story focus, even if they change along the way, will make your story more understandable (and thus more appealing!) to a potential editor.

So how do you take your topic and turn it into a story? All it takes is a bit more research to find the details you need. That said, your story hasn't been accepted yet—you don't want to invest the time and effort of reporting on the story in full before you've sold it. You have to be smart about your research time and get to the heart of the story quickly. This is where you do some preliminary digging—thanks to your friend, the pre-interview.

The art of the pre-interview

In school, and caught between multiple classes, assignments, and other responsibilities, you may have skipped the step of doing a pre-interview. But, as a freelancer, quick phone pre-interviews will save you a lot of time in your reporting, and give your pitch the focus it needs to sell it properly. Simply put, a pre-interview is a short interview, usually by phone, that gives you a chance to speak to a source while you're still in the planning and research stage of your story. It's a chance to chat up your source and find out

1. Their version of the story (does it align with what you thought the story was?)
2. Any background or contextual information that will help you frame the story
3. Whether or not your source is a good talker—especially important for audio or video interviews!
4. Whether or not they're open to a full interview should you go ahead with reporting the story

Typically, a simple 10-minute phone call with a potential main source for a story topic can help you turn it into a pitch.

If, during your research, you don't come across a main character, that's OK—look for a related expert as a first pre-interview. Not only will they give you much-needed context for your piece, they may be able to suggest potential characters.

Reaching out for a pre-interview is very similar to booking a regular interview, but in this case you will want to let the source know the context of the discussion—that this information is for a story that is in progress.

How to request a pre-interview

The best way to request a pre-interview is to send an email, though a phone call can work, too. A potential email request could look like this:

To: source@theircompany.com
From: youremail@yourwebsite.com
Subject: Interview request: your story topic

A Dear Mr. Source,

Hello! **B** I'm a freelance journalist **C** working on a story about X. **D** As you're an expert in the field, **E** I was hoping to talk to you to gain a better understanding as I develop the story further.

F I was wondering if you would be available for a quick phone call sometime this week? I would only need 10 minutes of your time at this point. **G** Wednesday and Thursday afternoon are quite flexible for me, though if another time works better for you, please let me know when is most convenient.

H Thanks, and I look forward to hearing from you,

Freelancer
Cell: 403-123-4567
Yourwebsite.com
Any other social media accounts

A Make sure to direct your email to your source—if possible, no generic inboxes, as they rarely get checked.

B You can choose to identify yourself as a journalist or a freelance journalist. If your story has already been approved by an outlet, you can let the source know what publication or show the piece is being produced for.

C Don't go into tons of detail, but give the source your story topic and focus so they understand what you're looking to do the interview about. Many experts are able to speak on many topics in their field, so knowing what information you're looking for is helpful for them.

D Flattery never hurts! If you have a specific reason why you want to talk to this expert, you can add this here, too. If your story connects to something that the source truly cares about and is involved in, the more likely they are to agree to the interview. Just try to not get too saccharine in your praise.

E It is essential to let your source know that this article is still in progress and doesn't have a set publication date. That said, avoid saying the story isn't going to be published, as that gives your source little incentive to speak to you (plus, the goal of the story is to eventually get published!).

F You'll notice that the email doesn't ask for a pre-interview—it asks for a 10-minute phone call during the week, which is a much clearer request.

G Offer some segments of time that work best for you, and of course let the source know that they can offer an alternative time that is more convenient. By providing some options, you're setting up for a situation where a source is much more likely to reply to you.

H Be polite, but encourage a reply. If you write "I hope to hear from you," that suggests that there's a chance they may not reply. Don't give your source an easy out!

Once you've booked your pre-interview, there are a few things to consider:

1. If you've asked for a 10-minute interview, respect your source's time. Prepare a few thoughtful questions accordingly and keep an eye on the clock.
2. Record your interview—and make sure to get your source's agreement on tape. Let them know how the tape will be used (e.g., on background, for publication).
3. Be clear in your requests if you're seeking a particular type of information. If you're looking for characters, other experts, or other places to dig further on the story, be sure to ask directly.
4. This is one of those interviews where asking "is there anything I've missed or anything you think I should know about this topic or story?" at the end can come in very handy—it might even take your story in a whole new direction.
5. Use this opportunity on the phone to confirm that your source is open to a longer, more fulsome interview if or when the story goes forward. Being able to include names of people in your pitch who have agreed to be part of the story is a great way to show a producer that you've done your research and know you can deliver on a story.

Writing and formatting your pitch

You have your story idea—a strong character, a good focus, and an idea of where it's going. You've done a few pre-interviews and feel confident in your idea. Now, it's time to craft your pitch ... BUT! Before you do, do yourself a favor and spend a few minutes doing an online search. Has this story been covered before? If it hasn't been—great! Onward!

Finding existing coverage of a story idea doesn't mean your story is a bad one—but you need to address it in your pitch, because the last thing you want is to email a big-shot editor saying you have a scoop only for them to find out via Google that their competitor had more or less the same story the previous week. If it has been reported—who covered it? When? Is there room for a follow-up? How can you rework your story idea so that it brings something new to the table? It's also worth checking to see where it was published—maybe that's where you can pitch your follow.

How you end up pitching a story depends on the outlet, the medium, and the story itself. But there are certain things the best pitches have in common:

1. They're short

No one likes to read a long email, so you want to craft an email that catches a reader's attention quickly, just like when you're writing an article. Include all of the salient details in your email, but take the time to ask yourself if a detail needs to be included in the email now—or if you can address it later if the editor follows up on your pitch.

2. They're focused

The point of your email is to sell a story—and, in small part, why you're the person to tell it. Other information can be included in future emails if (or when!) you hear back from the editor.

3. They're detailed

While this might seem like it goes against the first two rules, it's important that your pitch include enough detail to captivate the reader and prove that you have a good story with elements on which you can deliver. This means using your journalistic skills to carefully select details that serve your story and focus without turning your pitch into a novel. Include sources or characters if you have them, with short descriptions. Explain why the story matters and what's at stake. Short, bright writing doesn't just help sell your pitch—it shows your editor your skills as a journalist and what you can deliver in the final product.

4. They consider the outlet and the audience

One of the main complaints you will hear from editors is they get lots of pitches from people who have clearly never read, heard, or watched what they produce. While you don't necessarily need to explain WHY the story is a good fit if it's an obvious connection, you want to make sure that your pitch reflects the outlet and its audience. If you see the piece having things in common with something published a few months ago, reference that example. If you see your story being a good fit for a certain section of a magazine or a segment of a show, feel free to suggest it—it shows the editor that you're familiar with the work they do.

5. They take advantage of their medium

If you're pitching an audio piece, be sure to include what the listener will hear and what other sound elements will elevate the story and make it beautiful to listen to. Video pitches should describe at least part of what the viewer will see *and* hear. If you have compelling images or ideas for infographics for your print or online story, add them to your pitch. It shows you understand the medium you're pitching and are thinking about your story in a larger context.

Putting it together

The pitch you send will vary depending on the medium, the story, and your personal experience with the outlet or the producer. But here's an example of what a pitch email for a radio story might look like, based on an example from earlier in the chapter:

To: seniorproducer@dreamshow.com
From: youremail@yourwebsite.com
Subject: **A** Pitch: Naloxone and overdose deaths in Calgary

Dear Ms. Senior Producer,

B Hello! I'm a freelance journalist and recent grad from Mount Royal University's journalism program. My work has appeared in the Calgary Journal, the Calgary Herald, and BeatRoute Magazine—you can find my portfolio at mywebsite.com.

C I'm reaching out as I have a story idea that I think would be a great fit for your weekly series profiling people who are doing great things in the city: **D** since attending a community workshop last year on how to use a Naloxone kit, nursing student Renee Lavoie has administered the drug to complete strangers four times—and saved their lives. The piece will profile Lavoie, the lives she's saved from drug overdose, and how it's changed her future career plans.

E Specifically, I'd like to go with Lavoie to meet John Sanders, one of the people she saved three months ago. They haven't met since the night he overdosed at a house party, and they've both agreed to be recorded and interviewed for this radio story.

F I imagine this piece being a narrated mini-documentary-style piece with Lavoie and Sanders as the main voices, perhaps with an expert from the local public health unit as well, but would love to hear your ideas on what format might work best.

G Thanks for your time, and I look forward to hearing from you,

Freelancer
Cell: 403-123-4567
Yourwebsite.com
Any other social media accounts

Ⓐ Be clear in your subject that you're pitching a story—and a few eye-catching words of what it's about.

Ⓑ A brief line or two explaining who you are and some of the work you've done helps show the editor you have experience and are worth talking to. Your best outlets should be listed here.

Ⓒ Be clear that you're pitching a story, and if you have an idea of where it might fit in a show or a publication, mention it! If the story idea is influenced or a follow to something they've produced recently, be sure to reference that as well.

Ⓓ Your story idea, distilled into no more than a few strong sentences.

Ⓔ This is where you can add more detail to your pitch—in this case, it's describing what action will take place (Lavoie and Sanders meeting), why it's important (their first encounter since his overdose), and that both have already agreed to be interviewed (you've done your research!).

Ⓕ This is where you can briefly outline the technical elements of the piece—how long you imagine it might be, whether or not it's narrated, what format it might take. This will all likely change as you work with your editor, but a line or two helps show them that you've thought about how you would tell the story.

Ⓖ A polite way to say that you're waiting on a reply!

Ask a journalist: Editors tell you what they look for in a great pitch

While successful pitches vary depending on the medium, the story, your own personal writing style, and where you're pitching, here are some general guidelines that will help editors notice your pitches—from the editors themselves.

First and most resoundingly—know where you're pitching!

"Editors can tell in two seconds if you're just firing off pitches to everybody or you're firing off this pitch to several publications," says Jeremy Klaszus, editor-in-chief of The Sprawl, a locally-focused slow news pop-up in Calgary, Alberta.

That's why it's essential to tailor your pitch to the show or publication and demonstrate how your idea and skills will work with what they do.

Vivian Le is a producer with the podcast 99% Invisible, and she looks for pitches that reflect the show's focus on narrative, with character-driven stories that reflect on a bigger story or issue.

"We prefer pitches to be a page of very concise narrative. And so, if the pitch itself is written in an interesting and creative way, and it's clear and it's concise, that is one of the best things I think that you can do as a freelance pitcher," she says.

"I can tell when a freelancer knows our show and understands what we're looking for, and understands the difference between talking about a topic and talking about a narrative story. Because what we do is narrative storytelling, even though it sounds like we have a very design-specific show," says Le.

"People will tell us, 'Oh, here's this cool lake design thing.' And the limit is that it's kind of a cool thing—but what is the beginning? What is the middle of, what is the end of that story that you're going to take us through in that episode? That's what we're looking for."

Eli Lopez, senior editor of global opinions at the Washington Post, says the best way to show that you understand an outlet is to frame your pitch within what the publication has already covered.

"I think the key thing is a good pitch based on your knowledge of what the editor will find interesting and complimentary to what they've been doing," he says.

"One of the best things I can get is an email that says, 'Hey, I'm (your name), I'm working on this piece about (blank), I noticed that you wrote this argument a few months ago. I have something different that hasn't really been said, and I thought you might find interesting, it's attached. And that's, basically, the perfect pitch—if it comes with all the elements (of) why I should care, why is it different from what we've had before?"

Klaszus agrees and says a bit of kindness doesn't hurt, either.

"When I hear from somebody who's like, 'I've been following The Sprawl, I've been reading it, I liked this story. Here's what I've been thinking and here's a story that I think might fit'... A bit of flattery goes a long way, let's put it that way," he says.

If you're worried about pitching with little experience, the editors say focus on crafting a good pitch—that's what will get you noticed, not your resume.

"Our show actually works with a lot of early producers; we're not super scared of first-time producers. When I pitched, I was a first-time producer, too," says Le.

"As long as you have an interesting style and we think that you are sharp and can pick up the technical skills easily, we'll work with you to help you develop those kinds of skills. Because the actual production, recording someone, that's the easiest part of making a radio story. But if you know how to structure an interesting piece, that's the hardest part to teach."

When it comes to pitches for opinion pieces, Lopez says experience with the topic trumps journalistic experience.

"Honestly, I really don't care about the experience as long as the person knows what they're talking about and everything in the piece is backed up by facts and research," he says. "As long as you have the expertise, individually, and you show that on your piece and you have a very firm grasp on what you're writing about, it really doesn't matter."

So, if the pitch is your ticket in, how else can you craft a compelling sell? Klaszus, who did a mix of freelance work for more than a decade before starting The Sprawl, says it can help to put yourself in your editor's shoes.

"The biggest thing for freelancers, I think, is are you solving a problem for an editor? Because if you are, that goes a long way," he says.

That means pitching something that hasn't been covered or that hasn't gotten coverage lately or locally. It also means following directions, like word count.

"Some writers would rather just give the whole thing and then have the editor cut it, which makes more work for the editor. So, I know if I have a writer who can file 500 words of clean copy that's cut down, that's vastly preferable."

This also means carefully reading submission guidelines and making sure your pitch meets the criteria—after all, if you can't follow criteria in the pitch, how will you convince the editor that you will in your work? Many places will ask for different things ... and for Lopez, he's looking for more than a pitch.

"Drafts are better than pitches," he says. "If you have something already in the works that meets our specs, that's always ideal."

Lopez isn't looking for a fully completed, perfectly crafted piece of work—even a handful of paragraphs can help him see your writing style and determine if your argument is cohesive.

Does the idea of writing before you get the job make sense in terms of a fully reported story that requires interviews? Not at all. But in the case of opinion pieces,

where the format is pretty consistent and original reporting is minimal, Lopez says that even a few paragraphs
of a very rough draft can help sell him on a piece. It will
also make the editing process much faster, especially if the
piece is on a time-sensitive topic.

"Presenting a draft along with your short pitch [via]
email ... increases your chances, because if you are actually
within that perfect timeframe of when something is relevant, then we don't want to waste time and going back
and forth—you know, me telling you, 'Well, I need to see
a draft,' and then you get back to me an hour later," says
Lopez. "It gives a much more tight timeframe to get it
through that window."

And, if the editor passes on the piece, you're now in a
better position to go elsewhere.

"In my experience, when you present a draft, it gives
you a better option to shop it around. Even if you get
a rejection, you can move on to another publication," he
says. "And that's on us as editors to respect the freelancer's
time and try to respond as soon as possible, so they can
have the opportunity to go to another publication."

On that topic—should you send your pitch to several
places at once? The perhaps not-too-surprising answer
is no.

"If you send me a piece, don't send it to the Wall Street
Journal at the same time," says Lopez. "I don't want to
hear, 'Oh, I'm so sorry, it was the Journal that said yes
before you.' And you know what, that will get you banned
from a lot of publications—especially if we liked it. And
you'd be surprised, it happens a lot."

Instead, Lopez suggests picking one outlet and giving them a time frame to reply before you shop the story
elsewhere. "We want to hear that this is the first place
you've sent it to, but if you don't hear from us by the end
of the week, you're going to send it somewhere else," he
says. "That's fine."

As soon as the outlet is taking your story, it's time to talk about payment.

"If we move on to the next step and I say, 'I like this, I'd like to use it'—then you can immediately say, 'Oh great, how much are you usually paying for pieces like this?'" says Lopez. For a first piece, he says there may not be much wiggle room, but there may be opportunities to negotiate a higher rate for future pieces, particularly if you have a well-developed social media network where you promote your stories.

"It's always fascinating to me when freelancers never ask, or they ask at the very end, or I have to tell them that I will pay them," says Lopez. "As a freelancer, that's your livelihood, you should always ask and establish the price [upfront]."

Once you've worked out the expectations and price of the piece, that doesn't mean your communication with the editor is over. Throughout the process, it's important to reach out if you have any questions or the story starts to change. If you're having issues in your reporting, talk to your producer or your editor.

"Communication is really important when it comes to working with freelancers, because the worst case scenario is that, you know, a freelancer doesn't want to tell you that they're having these problems and the due date comes up," says Le. "And then you're both kind of stuck in a bind because the freelancer doesn't have what they need and it's too late for us to help them."

Le says to send an email to your producer or book a quick phone chat right when problems arise. "It's teamwork when we work with freelancers, so we want to help them problem solve these things. And the problems that they have are probably problems that we as producers or editors have had in the past, too. We have certain skills to help them work through these issues."

Whether it's an issue with a source, trouble booking an interview, or technical issues in editing, Le says the problem probably isn't as big as you think it is.

"I understand that fear completely, about not wanting to show your cards if you feel like you're not quite delivering. But you both—the freelancer and the editor— have the same goal of making a great piece. So that kind of communication is really important."

Klaszus agrees and adds that editors were a great resource while he was working freelance.

"I would say to my editor, 'I've done all these interviews. Here's what I think, here's where I think this is going, but I'm not sure.' And she would really help me work through that, because she would have fresh eyes, she wouldn't have been looking at it for a week," he says.

"Take advantage of your editors and check in. Especially in journalism, you don't know what you're going to find out, so don't be ashamed if you don't know something or you're stuck. That probably just means you're on the right track."

After all, you aren't just producing a story; you're also building relationships—ones that can help you secure more work and perhaps bigger projects down the line.

"It starts small. It starts with one story, right?" says Klaszus. "And then it's like, 'Oh, that was a good story. Okay. Do you want to take this other story?' You become part of the mix, you become part of the freelance roster."

Lopez agrees. While he usually doesn't have time for informational interviews, he says that when freelancers make a great pitch and work well with him to turn it into a good piece, he can make the time to talk.

"When I decide to build a relationship with a free-lancer over time, that's probably going to be built on the fact that that person got a really solid draft through me," he says.

Following up

If you hear back from the editor that they're interested in your piece—congratulations! If this was an editor you had an informational interview with, you will have a general idea of the process at their publication for freelancing, but this is the time to make sure that you understand what is expected and when it needs to be delivered. You will likely have a call with your editor to confirm the story's focus, length, and any other details that need to be worked out—typically, the outlet will want to change some elements from what you pitched to fit their needs, so be sure to note any changes in the plans and check to see if they're doable on your end. You'll also want to confirm how, when, and how much you will be paid for the piece. We'll talk more about these discussions in upcoming chapters.

If you receive an email from an editor saying they aren't interested in taking your story, that's OK, too. If any constructive advice on the pitch is included, keep it in mind for next time—but the truth is, many fine pitches aren't the right fit for a publication at a given time for a variety of reasons. If the story isn't time-sensitive, you know you can now retool the pitch and send it elsewhere.

In many cases, you won't get the clarity of an email saying no to your pitch—you probably just won't get a reply. This puts you in a gray zone, as usually it's frowned upon to send a pitch out to many outlets at once. If the story isn't time-sensitive, you may want to give an editor a few days to a week before following up. After a follow-up and a week or so, it is likely safe to say that you're able to move on and pitch to another place. If the story is time-sensitive, follow Eli Lopez's advice from above—you will still want to pitch to the outlet that's the best fit, but give the editors a time frame to reply before you shop it elsewhere.

It bears repeating that, in your freelance career, **you will have far more rejected pitches than successful ones.** That's completely normal—even the most successful freelancers have faced a good deal of rejection. It's understandable to feel disappointed,

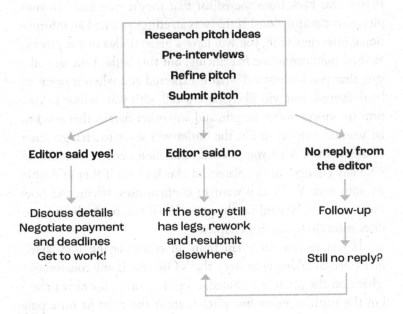

The Pitch Process

Research pitch ideas
Pre-interviews
Refine pitch
Submit pitch

Editor said yes!   Editor said no   No reply from
                                                  the editor

Discuss details   If the story still   Follow-up
Negotiate payment   has legs, rework
and deadlines   and resubmit
Get to work!   elsewhere   Still no reply?

but what separates successful freelancers from those who give up is how you decide to handle the "no." Will you take that experience as a learning opportunity and keep pitching?

At the end of the day, pitching is a numbers game—the more pitches you have out in the world, the better your odds are that one gets picked up. The more you practice and refine your pitches, taking feedback from editors and colleagues, the better they will be—which also improves the chances an editor will accept them. And, as you produce more great freelance work, editors will want to work with you again, and you will continue to build a portfolio that people will want to hire you for. It may not feel like it when you get your first rejection email, but it's all part of the process of building your freelance skills and your network. Tenacity is your friend.

A bit of forgetfulness can be healthy, too—a few years ago, I wanted to show some students my earlier pitch emails. A quick search in my inbox unearthed years and years of emails—some of them better pitched than others—most of them rejections or no-replies for projects I barely remembered sending out. While I'm sure you won't be forgetting any of your failed pitches right away, I can assure you that, in time, they will be fodder for your inbox archives while your resume and portfolio will be filled with the many stories that were accepted and went forward.

Time is money: Pitching and working efficiently

We know that, as freelancers, our income is directly linked to pitches that are accepted—that we then produce and publish. As we discussed above, the chances of having a successful pitch is directly linked to the number of pitches out in the world. Quality is important, but so is quantity.

On the other hand, you don't get paid for the work you put into a pitch unless it's accepted. As you likely know from experience, pitches don't just come out of thin air—they take time, research, and some concerted effort to polish up and present. If you don't watch your time or scheduling, it is entirely possible to spend your days crafting careful pitches ... days that you may not see a paycheck for. That's why it's important to plan your work around pitching as efficiently as possible.

Every freelancer you talk to will have a different way to plan and run their pitching work. But, regardless of your system, you'll want to decide on a way to keep track of what pitches you send where, and if/when you hear back. This will help you see what ideas you have on the go, when to follow up, and when to move pitches along to other outlets. A spreadsheet is a simple way to keep track of what's coming in and going out, and a good way to remind yourself of where things are as you start to have more and more projects on the go.

In terms of balancing pitch preparation and research so they don't take up all of your time ... again, it will depend on your schedule and what systems work best for you. Some journalists schedule a set amount of time every day to develop pitch ideas and follow up on emails; others may do it a few times a week or weekly. If you have a few freelance stories you're working on, you will likely be prioritizing those—whereas if you don't have any pieces on the go, you might want to spend a bit more of your time developing and sending out new pitches.

Ultimately, you want to work toward a workflow where you're pitching enough to bring in consistent amounts of work that you can deliver in the time you have available. Admittedly, this isn't an easy process, and one that freelancers constantly battle. Some months will be better than others, depending on the news cycle, annual budgets, and whether outlets are interested in your pitches. You may find that a regular client ends up taking in less freelance work for a few months, or that a show wants to hire you for a series unexpectedly. You will always be balancing the pitches going out with the work coming in, and so having all of that information in one place will help you make better decisions as you build your schedule and take on deadlines.

Can you deliver on that?

When a pitch is accepted, you probably want to jump straight to the enthusiastic yes—after all, that's why you pitched the story, right? But an important question to consider before you commit to the project is whether or not you can actually deliver on it. Accepting the work is committing to delivering on a final product, and it helps to make sure that, now that the pitch is being realized, it's feasible to complete.

For example, the producer might want some changes in focus on the story. While a change to the length of the story is likely an easy shift, perhaps they're looking for a different type of main character or a different angle on the topic. If you know that the story can still happen given those parameters, you're good to go— but if you're uncertain, be sure to bring up these concerns and explain what you might need to confirm to make sure the story will still work.

Aside from story content, take a look at the deadline and check your calendar—do you have any other deadlines at the same time? Upcoming projects? Shifts at your other job? If you need to shift a deadline to make the story happen, it's better to bring this up with an editor sooner rather than later.

The desire to say yes immediately is strong—understandably!—and you may feel that asking questions reveals that you're new or inexperienced. But the truth is, when you're freelancing, every story is unique, every outlet has their own way of doing things, and even different editors at the same place might run their departments differently. Even seasoned freelancers ask questions of their editors to make sure that everyone's on the same page and happy with the finished product.

Developing relationships, creating boundaries

While technically the output of your work as a freelancer is your story, the quality of your work depends on collaboration: with your editors or producers, with your sources, even with other freelance colleagues. That means that you should take the time to consider how you interact with people in your work—are you behaving in considerate and respectful ways that will encourage someone to want to work with you again?

Working respectfully with **editors** means communicating any issues you might have with your story as soon as it becomes an issue. While it might be stressful for you that things aren't going as planned—it happens often in our field—it's important to give the outlet time to work out alternatives or solutions. Any editor will tell you that they would rather hear about an issue with your story with lots of time to make adjustments instead of at the last minute, when there are limited options. Many times, the issue with the story is out of your control—like if a source isn't returning your calls. You can help your editor by providing alternative sources or angles for the story. If the issue with the story was your fault, like a missed deadline—own up, apologize, and provide some alternatives for the editor's consideration, i.e., a revised deadline that you can meet.

When in doubt, **ask the question.** If you're uncertain about word count for the story, avoiding an email might seem at first like you're doing the editor a favor, but it will be much more work for them in the long run if your piece is too long or too short. If a promised key source falls through, send a quick note explaining the change and what source you plan to use instead. If you're uncertain about file specifications or writing formats, see if there are any guidelines to follow. If you're worried about whether a question is wasting an editor's time, ask yourself: Will knowing this make my story better? Will it make it easier for my editor to vet? If the answer to either question is yes, it's worth a quick email. If you don't hear back, you can choose to push forward if it's a small issue, or send a friendly follow-up by phone or email in a couple of days if it's a significant one.

Working well with editors also means listening to their feedback and incorporating it into your work. Even the best drafts need revision, if only to incorporate simple changes so the piece fits the format and tone of the outlet. How well you address these edits is important—do you do what you're asked? Are you being defensive or argumentative about the changes? Are you asking for clarification when you're usure of an edit? Certainly, if the editor is suggesting a change that will make your story inaccurate or change the meaning of something, let them know. If you aren't sure how to make a specific change, ask for advice. But you want to make sure that you're helping make the editing process as clear and simple as possible.

The editing process is a time for you to show not only how great of a journalist you are, but that it's easy and enjoyable to work with you. If we go back to that image at the start of chapter 2, where you see yourself as an editor at a prestigious magazine—you're probably pretty busy, right? That's why editors like to work with journalists, freelance and otherwise, who are good at what they do, deliver a strong product on deadline that doesn't require a lot of editing, and make the revision process simple and straightforward. If you can provide all of this, there is a good chance you will find that editor hiring you for more work in the future.

Working respectfully with **sources** means communicating clearly the project you're working on and where and how their information will be used—and to follow up if any of those things change. This can be challenging, especially if you're pre-interviewing a source to develop a pitch that hasn't been picked up yet. That said, most sources are open to a quick phone interview if you're clear about what it's for and where you hope the story will go. Being transparent is essential, because you're relying on these sources to say yes to a full, proper second interview if the story in fact goes through.

Like in life, people appreciate it when you're on time, don't take too much of their time, and keep them in the loop of any changes that affect them. Put yourself in your source's shoes and ask what you would prefer in that situation. And sending a link to the story or showing when it's published is always a smart move. You may also find, as you publish more stories and interview more people, that sources will start coming to *you* with story ideas—one of the many rewards that comes with cultivating good relationships.

Beyond editors, there are many **journalists**—freelance or otherwise—who can help you navigate freelance work. They know what places take freelance pitches, can introduce you to colleagues in the know, and even help you figure out fair market rates for your work. Where you can, take the time to check in with other journalists, whether it's following up with people in your immediate network or joining online forums or groups for freelancing. There may be local journalist meet-ups in your area—ask around and see when or where they might be happening.

As we've discussed in this chapter, there's the organizational side of freelance work—developing and tracking where you send your pitches, balancing incoming projects while maintaining irons in the fire for future work, not to mention actually reporting and creating your work. There's also the interpersonal side of freelance work—connecting with editors and outlets, maintaining relationships with sources and colleagues, and navigating different editorial styles with each new project. It can be a see-saw, but with some planning and practice, you can create a system that works for you and the work you want to do. Rarely will you meet someone who loves both sides of the job equally, so acknowledge your strengths and weaknesses and create a plan that helps support you on the less-fun side of the job.

But there's a big piece of the organizational work of freelancing that we haven't touched on yet—the ins and outs of running yourself as a business. That's in the next chapter.

Jeremy Klaszus

writer and founder of The Sprawl

Freelance has been the common thread of Jeremy Klaszus's career since he graduated from Mount Royal University's journalism program in 2006.

First, it was pitching to local publications like Alberta Views magazine and alt-weekly Fast Forward (FFWD)—which later turned into an internship and a staff job at the paper. Then, Klaszus was back to freelancing for local publications before landing a job doing communications with the United Way. But, a couple of years later, he found himself back doing freelance journalism.

"I get restless after a couple of years, apparently ... And free-lancing, the thing I always liked about it, is I could combine that with other elements of life," he says.

"For example, when I left Fast Forward, my wife was going back to work after the birth of our first daughter. So it's like, okay, somebody needs to stay home or we have to find full-time child-care, and I found that I could really combine freelancing with being a stay-at-home parent. I could take on some assignments, I didn't have to overload myself."

Klaszus focused his freelance work locally, for the most part—though he has work published with the CBC, the Walrus, National Geographic Traveler, Vice, Metropolis, Reader's Digest, and the Globe and Mail.

With cuts hitting publications across the country, and with FFWD folding in 2015, opportunities in his hometown of Calgary for freelance reporting—as well as for independent or alternative news sources for readers—were starting to dry up. With his kids still in school, Klaszus wanted a flexible job that would allow him to continue to care for them after class. So he decided to use his freelance skills and reputation as a local writer and columnist to start his own news outlet, The Sprawl.

Klaszus started small, covering the 2017 municipal election with articles posted on Medium. He called it "pop-up journalism"—much like pop-up shops and events, the idea was to activate for big events or specific news coverage, with breaks in between to gather resources and work toward the next pop-up.

It was an experiment that exceeded his expectations: the initial plan wasn't to start crowdfunding, but a friend encouraged Klaszus to start a Patreon account during the first pop-up. By the end of the election coverage, there were more than 100 subscribers.

"And then there was, 'What happens next?' And I wasn't sure what happens next. That is part of the blessing and the curse of it," he says. He turned to his membership with three ideas for the next pop-up, and they overwhelmingly chose budget week at City Hall.

The Sprawl's slow-news values, pop-up esthetic and local focus has garnered lots of attention and support, from its 2,000-plus subscribers to major grants from organizations like Facebook's Journalism Project.

Klaszus credits their inclusive, content-first approach for the success they've found with crowdfunding.

"It's not like, 'Let's crowdfund and then I'll start doing this.' It's: 'I'll start. Here it is, covering the election, and please sign up to support this,'" he explains. "As journalists, we say, 'Show, don't tell' ... Well, that's exactly what I applied in this case in terms of building an audience and building a membership base."

And it doesn't hurt to focus on the positive.

"I think the paywall model is heavy-handed. It's like, 'We'll show you the article for two seconds and then we'll snatch it away and you'll have to pay if you want to view it.' It kind of leaves you with not a great feeling as a reader," he says.

"Our approach has always been, here's the story, here's the podcast, here's The Sprawl in its entirety that you have access to just like everybody else. And oh, by the way, we're crowdfunded, we're ad-free. And in order to do this, we need your support. So please consider pitching in."

The Sprawl has continued to grow and now hires local freelance journalists, putting Klaszus on the other side of the desk as an editor.

"It is weird to be on the other side now," he says. "I joke with my freelancers [that] I became the person I used to complain about—the editor that doesn't get back to you quickly."

It's business time

Freelancing is often described as working for yourself or being your own boss. While those aren't wrong descriptions, it misses a big part of the picture: as a freelance journalist, **you are the business**. And, just like other businesses you see out in the world—from coffee shops to design firms—you need to think like a business and run like a business.

Considering journalism is likely your passion (let's face it, you didn't get into this field for the money!), this can be a hard concept to wrap your head around. Journalism is a calling, is it not? What about the craft of storytelling? It can't just be about the money. That feels crass somehow. While it would be a wonderful world if we could simply live off our oeuvre, the truth is that you need to make a living. But it's about more than simply scraping by as a journalist—you have a set of skills that society needs, that many value, and that you can contribute to the bigger picture. Running yourself as a business is about being a professional that values your skills, sees what they bring to the world, and understands what you deserve in exchange for them.

Running a business doesn't mean you need to be the next Arlene Dickinson or Jeff Bezos. You don't need to rent an office or incorporate—though one day you might want to. Ultimately, running a business is

1. Understanding what you do
2. Figuring out how best to do it
3. Learning how much to charge
4. Making sure you get paid for it
5. Fitting your work into your bigger financial picture

As you can imagine, there are lots of ways that you can go about accomplishing those things, depending on your work and life situation. This chapter will go over some of the main concepts that can help you develop your business mindset, as well as some guiding questions to help you figure out what freelance options might be best for you. In the next chapter, we'll talk about specific ways you can put these ideas into action.

Yes, you can be a business

One of the first steps in building your business is recognizing and treating it as one. As someone who is new to the field, that might be an intimidating thought—after all, you're just starting out! It's a reasonable fear, but don't let that drive your decisions.

There are many narratives people create for themselves ... that they're bad with money, bad with math, not cut out for business. Maybe you've heard of imposter syndrome? It's the feeling that you are somewhere you shouldn't be, that you aren't qualified for your work; you fear being found out or called out by someone for it. It's incredibly common, particularly when you're starting out—do a web search, you will have reading for days! It's the kind of thing that can rear its ugly head, especially if you're taking a risk like going out on your own to freelance.

It's not a bad thing to be humble and to identify where you can improve in your work. But it's worth reminding yourself that you have trained and gained experience as a journalist. You have a portfolio! Just because you're new to the field doesn't mean you can't be a professional and shouldn't run your business as one, either. After all, if you don't see yourself as a professional, how will anyone else?

The other thing to remember is that your business *is a means to an end.* You want to tell great stories. You also want to pay rent and live your life and save up for the future. Running yourself as a business is a means to all of this; the business side doesn't have to be your lifelong passion. If you plan things well, you can create a system that works for you to let you do what you love.

> **When you doubt yourself ... ask yourself these questions:**
>
> 1. What is causing my doubt?
> 2. Is this based in past experience, or am I imagining a worst-case scenario?
> 3. What are my strengths as a journalist? What can I capitalize on?
> 4. What is some work that I've done that I'm proud of?
> 5. Who can I talk to that I trust to gain a better perspective on myself and my work?

No boss, no office, no benefits: The realities of freelance work

For most of us, the jobs we've had through school have been as employees. Maybe you worked at a coffee shop or a bookshop; perhaps you were a lifeguard at the local pool or waited at a restaurant. Regardless of your work, there were a few things you came to expect about getting paid as an employee:

1. You would get paid regularly (usually every two weeks).
2. You would be paid for the number of hours you worked, at a set wage.
3. Taxes, employment insurance, and other benefits would be deducted, meaning that the money in your check was essentially money you were free to spend.

As a freelancer, these "rules" no longer apply. Instead, it looks more like

1. You typically get paid when a project is completed or a work is published. This could mean many paychecks in one month and very few in others. Your checks will also likely vary in amount, compared to the more consistent ones you had before.
2. You will be negotiating different rates of pay for different projects; some will pay better than others.
3. As a contractor, your check is for the full amount of your work—you will be responsible for saving parts of your income for taxes come April, as well as saving for insurance, healthcare, and retirement.

You might be thinking that this feels like a worse deal than being an employee—and the research shows that, by the numbers, it is (see Nicole Cohen's *Writers' Rights: Freelance Journalism in a Digital Age* [2016] for more information). Generally, employees will make more money and reap more in overall income via company benefits. But there are advantages to working freelance as well. First, it can help diversify your work, meaning that you're not dependent on a sole employer who could let you go in tough times. It can also let you create a flexible work schedule instead of following 9-to-5 weekday hours, where you can take longer or more flexible vacation time than a traditional job. We'll get more into gig work and how it fits into the bigger labor picture in chapter 9, but what you need to know right now is that **freelance work requires a better understanding of your**

finances than when you're an employee. When you think about it, it comes back to *being your own boss*—the boss understands the whole picture when it comes to the business and its finances, even when the employees don't. And as a freelancer, that's you.

Let's look at how you can develop your business mindset. As mentioned, there are five main parts to consider as you plan your freelance business:

1. Understanding what you do
2. Figuring out how best to do it
3. Learning how much to charge
4. Making sure you get paid for it
5. Fitting your work into your bigger financial picture

Let's go through each of these concepts in brief, and the questions you might ask yourself to work out your plan.

Understanding what you do

This is likely the easiest thing to establish, if in fact freelance journalism is your goal! Perhaps you want to write features for magazines, or make radio documentaries, or produce web series for YouTube. Is there a certain niche or beat you want to focus on in your reporting? Your goals for what you want to do can and will shift, and that's OK. Start with what intrigues you and continue to refine as you go.

Figuring out how best to do it

This step is about taking the ideas you articulated in "Understanding what you do" and putting them into action. If you've already read chapters 2 and 3 about building your network and creating a plan for pitching and keeping track of your ongoing pitches, you're in good shape.

This is also where you set a plan for what your work looks like. Do you want to freelance full-time? Part-time, with a more steady part-time job to complement things? Do you want to keep at your full-time job and freelance off the side of your desk? Your goals might change as you gain more experience, but take some time to think about what your ideal freelance situation would look like at the start.

Understandably, money will likely influence your decisions here—so let's talk a bit about how to think about setting rates.

Learning how much to charge (aka figuring out your worth)

Talk to any freelancer and they will likely share that figuring out your rates is one of the toughest parts of the job. In the case of certain unionized shops, there are established rates for specific types of work. You can find both contractor rates and temporary employee hourly rates online through the union's websites. But, in most cases, you will be negotiating directly with your editor what you will get paid for a project—whether it be a flat fee for an article or project, a certain amount by the word, or an hourly rate for the work you do. Which begs the question: What's fair pay?

One of the best ways to figure out if a project is fairly priced is to calculate the number of hours, all-in, it will take you to complete it. This includes planning, researching, emailing, interviewing, transcribing, writing, recording, editing, revising, formatting, finalizing, uploading ... all of it. For example, let's say you're being offered 10 cents a word to write a 2,500 word feature. While $250 might seem like a decent amount (not a great amount, but a decent amount) for a project—how many hours of research and work would that project take?

For math's sake, let's say it would take about five hours a week over two to three weeks, putting the work in the 10- to 15-hour range. Take $250 and divide it by 15 hours—you're making about $16.50 an hour if you keep the project to that timeline. That's $16.50 an hour *before* tax—take off another 30 per cent at $4.95 an hour, and your take home pay is $11.55 an hour. Suddenly, that $250 paycheck doesn't seem so appealing. Of course, if you were able to do the project in a shorter time period—let's say 10 hours—you would be making $25 an hour. If you set aside 30 per cent for taxes, that comes to $17.50 an hour. But that assumes you can get the job done right in 10 hours, which as you likely know from experience just isn't feasible.

Knowing how much you will make hourly is an important part of deciding if a project pays enough—but how do you decide what a fair hourly rate is?

Generally speaking, a good way to do this is to look at the outlet or publication and see if you can determine what the average rates are for employees. For example, since the CBC is a unionized shop, you can go to their union website, the Canadian Media Guild, and click on CBC/Radio-Canada under "Our Workplaces" (you will see many other outlets listed too, if you're curious!).

By clicking on "Classifications and Hourly Salary Rates 2021," you will see that the hourly pay ladder for an entry-level associate producer (marked band 7) starts at about $27 an hour. That means that, if you were called in for a day to work as an entry-level associate producer, that is what you would get paid for your work ... so why would you take less in a freelancing contract?

As we will discuss later in this chapter, there are many things that you don't get when working freelance compared to being an employee—like health benefits, retirement savings plans, or unemployment insurance. That's why **you should charge more per hour than an employee** to cover those costs. While different people will give you differing advice, a good way to start the calculation is to add 50 per cent to an employee rate: 30 per cent for taxes and 20 per cent for unpaid benefits (we'll get to specific calculations later on). That means that, for a rate of $27 an hour, you would add $13.50, bringing your hourly rate to $40.50.

You might be looking at $40 an hour and thinking there's no way you could charge that, but it's important to remember that you have a useful set of skills that are worth a fair price. By being a contractor, you are already providing an essential service to a company at a lower rate than if they hired an employee. And I can also say with confidence that, in the world of audio-making, $40 for an hour's worth of quality work is still very much a bargain. If you're doing corporate work instead of news work, you'll want to consider raising your rates even higher.

Does this mean that it's reasonable to expect that rate for all of your projects? Unfortunately not. Looking back to the 10-cents-a-word rate from the example above—to make at least $40 an hour would involve writing that 2,500-word feature in about 6 hours altogether (and you likely know from your reporting experience that six hours might result in a feature, but not necessarily one worth printing!). Ten cents a word is a common rate for writers these days—particularly in print, where writers' incomes haven't increased in about 30 years, according to reports from the Professional Writers Association of Canada (which is now part of the Canadian Freelance Guild). While magazines will sometimes pay more, the gold standard in writing is often a dollar a word, and fewer and fewer publications are offering that rate these days.

There are ways to increase your income despite low rates, like researching a bigger topic or issue and using the information to create multiple pitches that you can sell as different articles to different publications, which cuts down on your research and preparation time. And sometimes you might want to take on a project, even if it doesn't pay well, to add a new outlet or type of work to your portfolio. In some cases, you might take on a project knowing that the hours won't work out great for pay *this* time around, but will become worth it as you get faster and gain more experience or are able to negotiate a higher rate next time. As long as you know your monthly budget, know your working worth, and know why you're taking on a project, you will be in a good position to make these choices.

One of the biggest struggles for freelancers in figuring out rates in the past was that they worked alone and negotiated directly with outlets—but now, thanks to the internet and freelancer-focused organizations, there are many places you can go to find out going rates. There are infinite online resources for you to discover, including, among others, Who Pays Writers (whopayswriters.com) and Media Bistro (mediabistro.com) for writers, and the Association of Independents in Radio (airmedia.org), which is a great resource for audio producers looking to work with US outlets. The Canadian Freelance Guild can also be a helpful tool for members looking for help to determine fair rates for their work. And don't forget your network—talk to freelancing friends and colleagues to help figure out what rates make sense for where you are.

Also worth mentioning—as you gain skills and a reputation for yourself as a freelancer, you can and should start to negotiate a higher salary. Don't be afraid to revisit your rates as you grow and have more to offer as a journalist. We'll talk more about how to negotiate in chapter 8.

Making sure you get paid for it

Questions that are a bit more administrative, but equally essential, include

- How will you work to get more comfortable talking about money and billing?
- How will you invoice for your work?
- How will you track your invoices and income?
- How will you approach clients who haven't paid you?

You probably don't like to talk about money. It's OK, most people don't! But it is essential to do so if you want to, you know, actually *get paid* for your work. My advice around the money talk is to think of it like asking those tough questions in an interview: smile, do it in a friendly way, and keep at it until it feels second nature. Just like asking those tough questions is part of the job of a journalist, talking about money is the job of a freelancer. And while you may have been raised to think that money is considered taboo to discuss, remember that this is your job—not a polite conversation at a dinner party.

It's also worth noting that **editors expect you to talk about money**. It's part of their job to negotiate rates and pay freelancers—along with assignments and editing, of course. So don't worry about offending their sensibilities. In fact, payment should be what you discuss with your editor *right after deciding on the story and work you'll be providing*. This is because it will help you in

1. Determining the scope of work, since your pay is often tied to the length of your piece—i.e., by the word in written articles or by the minute for a radio documentary;
2. Understanding how much you'll be paid, which helps you decide how much time you should be investing in a project; and
3. Deciding whether or not to take on a project, based on the pay, deadlines, and scope of work.

Talking about money upfront also gives you an opportunity to ask how and when you will be paid, which will help you plan your personal income around multiple projects and varying paychecks.

Part of ensuring you get paid is sending out clear, complete invoices that help you get paid on time—and keeping track of them somewhere safe and accessible. You'll also want to keep track of who has paid you and when, so you can follow up on late payments if need be. We'll delve into the specifics of how to do this in the next chapter.

Fitting your work into your bigger financial picture

This is a category that will look a bit different to everyone, but it serves an essential role—mapping out a plan that works both for your work and your finances. Specifically,

1. How much do you need to make monthly to live?
2. How much do you think is feasible to make from freelancing?
3. What gear do you have, and what do you still need? How much will that cost?
4. What other costs will you incur monthly for freelancing? Can that be covered by your income?
5. What is your plan for setting aside money for taxes?
6. How will you cover health, insurance, or other monthly or unexpected costs?
7. Do you have an emergency fund to help cover the slow months?
8. Do you have a plan for where or how to save during the best months?
9. Will you need a side job to help make enough money?

You won't have answers to all of these questions right away, but they're ones you will need to answer early on in your freelancing career. Like most things, you can always refine your plans as you go.

As a boss running your own business, you'll need some strong personal finance knowledge to figure out a financial plan for what you need to live off of as a freelancer. Understanding what your monthly budget looks like, making sure you set aside money to pay taxes, and developing an emergency fund and a plan for future savings are all at the core of making sure that you benefit financially while working freelance. These are also great skills to have just in general, but they will definitely provide a strong foundation for running a business. Once you have an understanding of your personal financial needs, you'll be in a better position to understand what you need to run as a business. I will say this again because it bears repeating: **You don't need a perfect plan or to have everything figured out before you start your freelance career.** You will figure out a lot along the way! But being aware of these issues and having an idea of where to get help will save you from some unpleasant surprises in the future.

Figuring out your personal finances

Having a strong sense of your money—what you have, what you owe, and what you need to cover your expenses—is the first step in understanding your finances on a bigger level. Like most freelancers, you will likely start out as a sole proprietor, meaning you aren't incorporated, and your business income is tied to your personal income, with taxes filed through your personal accounts. Because your personal and business accounts are inextricably tied, it's important to understand your finances as you plan to work freelance.

Erin Lowry is a New York-based freelance finance writer and author of the Broke Millennial book series, and her specialty is helping new and young professionals plan their finances. Here's her advice to those looking to step into the freelance world—starting with the question at the heart of it all: **How much do you need to make monthly to live?**

To accomplish this, Lowry suggests that you start with a **bare essentials budget**. This means calculating the absolute basics you need to live for a month. This could include

- Rent/shelter
- Utilities—remember to include internet and your cell phone!
- Transportation—bus fare, taxis, or gas and the other costs associated with your car
- Food
- Any monthly healthcare costs
- Any debt payments

This is the absolute lowest amount of money you need to make in a month to break even.

But wait—one last calculation! Since taxes aren't taken off your paycheck, you will need to set that money aside for tax time.

Add 30 per cent to your amount (a rough estimate of what you will owe to the government).

For example, a bare essentials budget might look like this:

Rent	$750
Utilities ($75 electrical, $50 heat, $75 internet, $75 cell phone)	$275
Bus pass	$125
Groceries	$450
Healthcare coverage	$250
Student loan repayment	$150
Total	$2000
Add 30% for estimated taxes (multiply by 0.3)	$600
Total minimum monthly budget	**$2600**

This budget is your **basic monthly costs**—it doesn't include eating out, drinks with friends, going to movies, buying clothes, or other hobbies or creature comforts. You will also make a budget that includes these things to have an idea of what you would like to aim for monthly, but for now let's focus on the baseline.

Once you have your bare essentials budget, you have the answer to the question of **how much do you need to make monthly to live?** That then leads to the next question: **How much do you think is feasible to make from freelancing?**

For some ideas on how to plan rates, head back to "Learning how much to charge" earlier in this chapter. But, to get an idea of the practical going rates in your area, Lowry suggests you talk to your contacts in the field who are also relatively new to freelancing. Ask about their rates, the work they're doing, and what a reasonable amount of work to expect monthly would be. It won't be exact, but it will give you an idea of whether or not you will be able to make ends meet each month—which is a good place to start.

Considering a second job

And what if you can't make ends meet on freelance alone? That's not the end of the world—and to be honest, many freelancers don't, particularly when starting out. It just means you'll need to consider another income stream for the time being. Some freelancers serve as contributing editors part-time to create a steady paycheck; others teach or tutor; others have a job outside of journalism altogether. When you're just starting out, Lowry points to part-time serving or retail jobs as a way to have a steady paycheck that provides the flexibility to freelance—or perhaps you want to take on a full-time job to build up savings while you build your freelance network.

"I think that that's really a shrewd way to go about it in the beginning. And the reason I say that is not to be like, 'Oh, you're not going to make it as a freelancer.' It's ... the amount of brain space we spend stressing about money. When there's not enough money, it makes it really hard to write, to ideate, to create," Lowry explains.

"So if you can somehow alleviate that pressure for yourself—even 50 per cent—if you can have a job that's getting you 50 per cent of the way there, that just takes the pressure off of the kind of projects that you can take as a freelancer. And it will probably embolden you to be a bit better about negotiating early on, because you don't have to work from a place of scarcity."

While it's important to be able to cover your monthly costs, your goal with your career shouldn't be just to scrape by. So while knowing your absolute bottom monthly income is essential, remember that it's only the start! Here's what Lowry suggests are other things to consider as you continue to learn more about your personal finances.

Paying off debt

It's a tough thing to do, but you need to take a good look at the debt you owe, because it's the only way you'll be able to plan to pay it back. Lowry suggests taking a look at how much you owe in your last year of school and figuring out what those payments will look like once you're out of school. If you've graduated and still haven't looked, now is the time.

If you have loans from the government, Lowry suggests taking a look at loan repayment plans. "Look into an income-driven repayment plan," suggests Lowry. "That's then going to be tied to how much money you make. So you still have to make the payments, but they're probably not going to be as cost-prohibitive as they might otherwise have been."

If your student loans are through a private lender, like a bank, they are usually not as flexible on payment plans. You can always ask, but plan to prioritize those payments and expect that they will not change.

Paying for healthcare

If you're an American, you're likely familiar with (and perhaps overwhelmed by) the many options for healthcare coverage and how it varies state to state—and it isn't cheap. If you're able, Lowry recommends staying on your parents' coverage until the maximum age of 26—"And then once you get the boot, look at the other options that are available to you based on where you live."

If you're in a situation where you need to buy your own coverage, put your journalistic research skills to use and do a lot of reading and asking questions before making a decision. National groups such as the Freelancers Union offer plan discounts for their members, as do many other unions that run nationally, state-wide, or more locally, depending on the type of freelance work you plan to do.

Lowry also suggests having the amount of your plan's deductible saved and set aside so that you will be in good financial shape should you need to use your coverage. A deductible is the cost to you when you use your medical insurance, and can vary from hundreds to thousands of dollars depending on your plan.

In Canada, healthcare is publicly funded, meaning that there is no requirement to have additional health coverage beyond Medicare. But there are a lot of healthcare services not provided through Medicare, like vision care, dental care, prescriptions, or ambulance trips. Depending on your health situation (and your finances), it may make sense to buy additional coverage through a provider. Again, this is where your journalistic research skills can come into play to figure out what provider and what level of coverage might work for you. The Canadian Freelance Guild offers access to healthcare coverage to its members, which may be worth considering, as well.

Having an emergency fund

Whether you're enjoying a regular paycheck or not, most financial planners will encourage you to create an emergency fund. As you may guess by the name, this money is for emergencies—like your car breaking down, losing work, or a family emergency. And yes, it has to be a separate account (otherwise it's tough to fight the impulse to spend!).

The general guidance for an emergency fund is three to six months of your bare essentials—in fact, that's what Lowry used to recommend. But now, she's changed her mind.

"I mean, ideally you have at least six months of bare essential living expenses, but that number just sounds so outrageous to most people when you're starting out. A great number is one month bare essential living expenses. And I would tack your healthcare deductible onto that. If you want to lay a strong foundation and then continue to build, I will say that six-month number ... but it just feels so overwhelming at first, so aim for a month as you get started, especially if you're self-employed, because income will be volatile."

If we go back to the bare-bones budget that was $2600, that would mean your first goal would be to save $2600—though a longer-term goal could be three months' of expenses, which would be $7800. It's a lot of money—likely, more money than your savings account has ever seen—but it's worth it. Not only are emergency funds incredibly helpful when you're dealing with the costs of an emergency, but they can also help provide a sense of security as you navigate the uncertain path of being your own boss. Knowing that you have some money socked away in case things go wrong can alleviate the stress of living paycheck to paycheck, and while the idea of saving that money may seem like a burden at first, it will pay off in the long run by providing a sense of security and a bit of a safety net when things don't go to plan. A fully funded emergency account may take years of saving to accomplish, but you can get there bit by bit.

Saving for retirement

You might be thinking that you're so busy trying to get *into* the job market that it's too soon to plan for retirement. Saving for retirement may be tricky at first, but you'll want to start planning and putting away money sooner rather than later. Unless you plan on finding a full-time job with a pension, you will need to be saving for when you retire (and honestly, you still need to save even if you have one of those rare pensioned jobs!). The general advice is to put aside 10 per cent of your paycheck to retirement—and it's a great goal, but even if you're putting in less at the start, you'll be creating the habit for when you make more money (and you will start making more money!).

In Canada, the best-known stream for retirement savings are registered retirement savings plans (you may know them as RRSPs). RRSPs are often quite popular because of the tax savings: the account is tax-deferred, which means you won't pay taxes on the money you put in the account, which means a better tax return for the year. That's the deferral part—you pay the taxes when you're retired instead, and since you'll likely be making less money, you will play less in tax.

This can be a great tool, but it only really works for you if you're making good money and in a higher tax bracket. That's why some advisors recommend saving your money in a tax-free savings account (TFSA) early on in your career, and then moving to saving in RRSP accounts later, when you make more money and will save more on taxes. Doing your research and even booking an appointment with a fee-for financial planner can help you figure out what makes the most sense for your situation and savings. We'll talk more about financial planners in chapter 6.

In the United States, individual retirement accounts or arrangements (IRAs) are the main vehicle to save for retirement. There are many options, from the traditional or Roth IRAs—but, if you are self-employed, you also have the option to contribute to a simplified employee pension (or SEP) IRA. There are advantages to different IRAs depending on your work and finances—you will want to dive in, do some research, and consider an appointment with a fee-for financial planner, who can help you figure out what makes the most sense for your situation.

Saving for other fun things

Of course, savings don't just apply to emergency funds and retirement. Maybe you'd like to save for an annual vacation, or put a bit of money aside for the holidays so that you don't get hit with an unpayable credit card bill in January. You can definitely create an account and/or automate any additional transfers for savings, and there are many ways you can go about setting that up. It's another way to keep an eye on your money and make sure that you can have some fun or take some time off without throwing your budget.

Revising your budget

Earlier in this chapter, we looked at a bare essentials budget. But, as you grow your income and are ready to add savings and future planning to the mix, your budget could look more like:

Rent	$750
Utilities ($75 electrical, $50 heat, $75 internet, $75 cell phone)	$275
Bus pass	$125
Groceries	$450
Eating out, movies, other monthly fun activities	$250
Healthcare coverage	$250
Student loan repayment	$150
Emergency fund savings	$100
Retirement savings	$75
Vacation/fun savings	$75
Total	$2500
Add 30% for estimated taxes (multiply by 0.3)	$750
Total minimum monthly budget	**$3250**

OK, but how do I save money when my paychecks are so variable?

The thought of saving money when you have no idea how much money you will make in a month might feel impossible—it did for me when I started out. Luckily, there are many books out there that can help you with different tips and techniques for managing your money even when it's inconsistent.

Personally, *The Money Book for Freelancers, Part-Timers and the Self-Employed*, by Joseph D'Agnese and Denise Kiernan, was an eye-opening read when I started working freelance (though admittedly some of the chapters are less applicable to Canadian workers). Specifically, the idea of saving *percentages* of my paychecks to different savings accounts—sort of a digital version of envelope saving—helped me create a savings plan even for when I had only a bit of money to save. For example, early on I would put 30 per cent of each paycheck into a savings account for taxes, 7 per cent to my student line of credit that I took out for journalism school, and 3 per cent to my emergency fund. For a $100 check, that was only $10 going to the line of credit and emergency fund, but for a $1000 check, that was $100—and it added up much more quickly than I anticipated. Once my line of credit was paid off, I took the 7 per cent I was putting to the line of credit and bumped up my emergency fund to 5 per cent, then created two new accounts for saving: a vacation savings fund in which I put 2 per cent of each paycheck, and a retirement/long-term savings fund to which I contributed 3 per cent.

The unexpected win of this system, for me, was that I now paid much more attention to when money was coming in, as I had to organize and transfer the right amounts. It was a fun way to recognize the hard work it took to get started as a freelancer—in many ways as satisfying as those first bylines or the thrill of hearing a national radio host introduce my piece on-air. As I met certain goals—like paying off the line of credit—I could move on to other savings goals and adjust percentages as needed. If I had a check that needed to go straight to rent, I didn't beat myself up over those missing savings because I knew that, for the most part, I was putting aside what I needed. And, at the end of the tax year, if I'd over saved for taxes, then there was a nice cushion I could transfer to my other savings goals (and maybe something nice for myself, too!).

We all work differently in how we manage money—and a lot of our attitudes toward work, money, and savings are tied to how we grew up. It can be a complicated and sometimes emotional thing to navigate, and there's no one right way to do it. I encourage you to use your research skills to find some books, sites, or even credible social media accounts that can help you get more comfortable thinking about money, talking about money, and planning how to use your money. After all, once you have a better understanding of how finances work and how to align them best with your work, lifestyle, and values, you will be in a position to make informed choices—a much better alternative to feeling weighed down and controlled by your finances, or stressing out every year when taxes are due.

The good news is that, as the field of freelancing continues to grow, so are services and organizations designed to support the self-employed. Be sure to look for groups that can guide you in business and financial planning, as it can be a great source of information and a way to develop your freelance network. Some of these organizations have membership fees, but can also provide discounts on health coverage or insurance plans. Another option is to find online courses from reputable sources—for Canadian freelancers, the New School of Finance offers courses in starting your own business and what you need to know. In the United States, the Writers' Co-op offers a free podcast, as well as paid coaching sessions and courses that can help you start your freelance business.

When beginning to plan your finances, the cost of an advisor might seem daunting—but a short investment in getting the right information now can save you a lot of time, money, and stress later. Booking an appointment with a fee-for financial planner can help you better understand your finances and how to keep track of what you need for your first tax filing as a freelancer. We'll be talking more about taxes in chapter 6.

Financial planning resources

As you continue to research and develop your business and money mindset, here are but a few books that may be a good start:

American resources

Broke Millennial: Stop Scraping By and Get Your Financial Life Together, Erin Lowry (2017)

The Money Book for Freelancers, Part-Timers and the Self-Employed, Joseph D'Agnese and Denise Kiernan (2010)

The Freelancer's Bible: Everything You Need to Know to Have the Career of Your Dreams—On Your Terms, Sarah Horowitz and Toni Sciarra Poynter (2012)

Canadian resources

Worry-Free Money: The Guilt-Free Approach to Managing Your Money and Your Life, Shannon Lee Simmons (2017)

Moolala: Why Smart People Do Dumb Things with Their Money—and What You Can Do About It, Bruce Sellery (2011)

Stop Over-Thinking Your Money! The Five Simple Rules of Financial Success, Preet Banerjee (2014)

Once you have an understanding of your money and what you need to cover your bare-essentials costs (and hopefully save for other important and fun things, too!), it's time to take a look at the mechanics of running a business—how to put your plan into action.

Erin Lowry

financial writer and author of the Broke Millennial series

When Erin Lowry graduated with a degree in theater and journalism in 2011, she came into a job market that was still recovering from a recession.

"I did a combination of applying to a lot of journalism-focused jobs, usually broadcast," she says. "I had a reel and I was sending it to stations ... 70 applications and maybe heard back from two places."

It was looking like her best job option was to work at the bookstore in her hometown of Charlotte, North Carolina—"And even they didn't end up calling me back after the interview! It was [a] pretty bleak time."

A week after graduation, Lowry got a call from the "Late Show with David Letterman." They had received her application to be a page on the show ... and a few weeks later, she was on her way to live and work in New York City. Along with her job on Letterman, she worked as a barista and a babysitter to make ends meet.

It was exciting to see behind the scenes of the entertainment industry, but it was exhausting.

"I was honestly feeling so burned out and just wanted a steady paycheck and just couldn't bear the thought of continuing to try to 'make it.'"

Lowry used connections with a friend working in public relations to land a job with an agency. The full-time gig meant she had a bigger salary, health insurance, and a matching a 401k plan. The catch: she hated the work.

"It's nothing against PR," she explains. "It just was not a good fit for me and what I wanted."

Lowry was missing writing and needed a creative project—so she started up Broke Millennial, a financial advice blog, that she ran off the side of her desk while working PR. From there, she moved to work with a fintech start up, where she ran their blog. Then, the offer came for the first Broke Millennial book.

"I did what they always tell first time authors *not* to do ... I quit my day job!"

While it was a big jump, Lowry had a plan. "I had built up my freelance writing portfolio while I was working day jobs so that, when I made the leap, I already had a very strong base and a very big savings net in case anything went sideways."

Lowry has been working freelance full-time as a writer and speaker since 2017—a far cry from where she thought she would be when she walked across the stage at graduation.

"I had to have had a concept that freelance was a thing, but I didn't really think about that as a genuine option. And I think [it was] because no one talked about it. It wasn't like, 'Hey, you can actually go out there and cobble together gigs and it will be enough to pay your bills,'" she says.

"And at the time, that would have felt like such a scary proposition, especially without really much of a portfolio."

Though she misses the employer-matched 401k, office tech support, and working with colleagues, Lowry points out that freelance comes with the benefit of multiple income streams and control over the work she chooses to do. It's also an opportunity to work with and learn from a mix of people across the field.

Lowry recalls one time where an editor returned one of her stories covered in red ink.

"I was feeling very cranky. And somebody said to me, 'Yeah, but if you think about it, with a really good editor, that's not only free advice, you're getting paid to get good advice on how to become a better writer.' Which I thought was such a great mental reframe," she says.

"You can work with some really wonderful editors and that's sort of like getting paid for having a masterclass in whatever you are learning."

Chapter 5:

Freelance business basics

In this chapter ...

- Negotiating the financial terms of your work
- Billing for services rendered and how to write an invoice
- Tracking who has paid you, how much, and when
- How to get paid, and what to do when you get paid

N ow that you're familiar with the main concepts related to running your own freelance business, this chapter is where we put those ideas into action. Specifically, as a freelancer, you will need to be familiar with

1. Negotiating the financial terms of your work
2. Billing people and places for services rendered
3. Tracking who has paid you, how much, and when

Each of these steps is pretty straightforward, and there are a few ways you can go about accomplishing them.

Negotiating the financial terms of your work

As we discussed in chapter 4, you will want to get comfortable talking to editors about what you will be paid very early on as you agree on the scope of the work you'll be doing—not only does it help you understand if a project is worth your time and effort, it will help you plan your finances.

Figuring out your pay is essential, but there's more to know than just the money. You'll want to ask *how* you get paid. Most organizations will request an invoice after you've delivered on your work—it's worth asking if there are any special requirements for the invoice itself, and where it should be submitted. Some types of work, such as hourly or temporary work, might require a timesheet, so you will want to make sure you have a copy, understand how to fill it out and where to submit. You will also want to find out how they will be sending your payment—by electronic transfer, by check—so that you can provide the necessary information (i.e., your account number or mailing address) to be paid promptly.

Some jobs will involve a contract, which you will need to read and sign (and negotiate any terms, if needed—we'll get to that in chapter 8), and others will be an agreement you come to with an editor over email or phone. Do your best to have everything in writing, and keep copies in your email to refer to if there seems to be a discrepancy between you and your editor.

Another thing you will want to discuss is a **kill fee**. This is the amount of money you will be paid if you deliver on the article and your side of the agreement, but the publication decides to not go ahead with publishing it. It's essential to have a kill fee as most journalists don't get paid until a story is published—no publication means no money for your work. Hopefully, your story won't require a kill fee, but it's best to have some sort of compensation if the story doesn't make it to print—particularly if you've invested a lot of time and effort.

Questions to ask an editor as you negotiate a project

1. Can we confirm a description of the work in writing, including length, deadlines, and any other expectations?*
2. What is the rate I will be paid for the work?*

3. When and how would you like me to invoice for the work? Are there any specifics to your system that I should know about?

4. Where and when should I submit invoices or timecards?

5. What is the kill fee for this project?*

denotes areas that can be negotiated, depending on the editor and the outlet

Billing people and places for the services you've rendered

As a business, billing is one of the first skills you'll need to practice and perfect.

"I would tell someone, first off, you need to keep track of the money that's coming in: who owes you money, who you owe money to, and keep track of your expenses. And you need to do that in a systematic way for two reasons," explains Jonathan Medows, the founder of CPA for Freelancers. "Number one, you have to keep score. And number two, you have to pay taxes. And if you're disorganized in your recordkeeping, specifically of people that owe you money, you may leave money on the table."

You'll hear more from Medows in the next chapter, when we talk about tax planning. But before you can pay your taxes, you have to get paid! As a freelancer, there are many ways you may communicate with outlets or companies to be paid, but the standard format will be to send an invoice. An invoice is essentially a bill for your work, which is usually processed by the accounting department, which in turn sends you your money.

How to write an invoice

There are lots of beautiful and complicated formats for invoices out there—just do a web search and you will be inundated! But the truth is, even though there are lots of fancy tools and software floating around the internet, an invoice can be as simple as

INVOICE

E Invoice Date:

A Your Name
Address, including
City, state, ZIP
B Email address

F Invoice Number:

C News Outlet
c/o Editor's name
D Address, including
City, State, ZIP

Description	Amount
G Story on pets and social media, 1000 words @25 cents/word	250.00
I GST @ 5%	12.50
TOTAL **H**	262.50

J Payment due by

K Please make cheques payable to Your Name

E-transfers can be sent to yourname@youremail.com

a Word document or PDF outlining a description of the work done and the basic information you need to get paid.

No one is paying you based on the aesthetic quality of your invoice—so keeping things clean and simple is often best. Regardless of format, your invoice should include

A Your name (and the name of your company, if you have one)

B Your address, including your email address

C The name of the outlet you are billing, with the name of your editor (unless the company specifies otherwise)

D The address of the company you are billing

E The date

F An invoice number (which you can make up—but it will help down the line for tracking purposes, as we'll get to in a moment)

G A short description of the work completed

H The amount owed for the work

I The amount of taxes owed (if you are collecting tax on behalf of the government, such as GST/HST [general/harmonized sales tax] in Canada, as in this example, or a sales tax for goods and services in the United States)

J A due date for the payment (30 days from it being issued is standard)

K Details on how to pay you—some companies will pay by e-transfer, which can be sent to a preferred email address. Others may need you to fill out a form with your account deposit information. Others will pay by check, so be sure to include your current mailing address on your invoice.

When you invoice depends on the project—for an article, you may invoice for the full amount after submitting the final piece. If you receive an advance on a project, you will invoice for the advance and then likely again at the end of the project for the remaining amount. There are many ways you can choose to invoice, as long as you and your client agree on the terms. For example, when I do hourly work for a client, I invoice at the end of every month. I also keep a running track of my hours with general descriptions of the work done and include it in my invoice as a sign of transparency (and to remind myself what I'm billing for if any questions come up!). You can see an example below. If you're billing for a single article or radio piece, identifying the project or slug and length is likely more than enough detail in your description.

INVOICE

Invoice Date:

Invoice Number:

Your Name
Address, including
City, state, ZIP
Email address

Client/Company
c/o Editor's name
Address, including
City, State, ZIP

Description	Amount
10 hours of audio editing @$45/hour (June)	450.00
GST @ 5%	22.50
TOTAL	472.50

Time worked

June 5: Editing puppies promo (2.5 hours)

June 10: Second-round edits (1 hour)

June 14: Rendering and uploading files (1.5 hours)

June 15: Editing kittens promo (2.5 hours)

June 21: Second-round edits (1 hour)

June 22: Meeting (1 hour)

Correspondence (.5 hour)

Payment due by

Please make cheques payable to Your Name

E-transfers can be sent to yourname@youremail.com

While invoicing might feel like a big business move, this is one part of your work you don't have to overthink—as long as your invoice is clear to read and has the information above, you should be in good shape. Make sure you save these files for your records.

Tracking who has paid you, how much, and when

Sending out invoices is the first step to getting paid—the next step is to set up for tracking your income, hours worked, and business expenses. This is how you will keep track of the bigger picture of your business, the information you need to plan your personal finances, and, ultimately, your tax filings. There is tons of software out there—some of it is even free!—but, just like a plain document works for your invoice, many professionals suggest you start simple and make a good old-fashioned spreadsheet.

What do you need to track? It will depend on the type of work you're doing, but here are some great places to start:

Track your invoices and income by creating columns with the date, the invoice number, a short description of the work, the amount charged, and a space to mark when the payment has been received (see the example below). This will also let you keep a running tab of your income, so you can more easily calculate your expected taxes and what you should be setting aside. It can also help flag when you are close to hitting an income threshold—for

	A	B	C	D	E	F
	Date	Client	Invoice	Amount	Work details	Received?
1	2022-01-30	Amp It Up Editing	AIU-2	$500.00	January billing	yes
2	2022-02-14	Localnews.Site	LN-1	$300.00	Transit story @15 cents/word	yes
3	2022-02-28	Amp It Up Editing	AIU-3	$650.00	February billing	yes
4	2022-03-07	LocalNews.Site	LN-2	$300.00	Taco stand battle @15 cents/word	no
5	2022-03-28	Glossy Magazine	GM-1	$1,000.00	Parks feature @$1/word	no
6	2022-03-31	Amp It Up Editing	AIU-4	$200.00	March billing	no
7						
8						
9	TOTAL EARNED			$2.950.00		

example, in Canada, if you've made more than $30,000 from freelance in the past 12 months, you're required to sign up for a GST or HST number. In the United States, you may need to collect sales tax depending on the freelance services you provide. We'll talk more about these additional taxes in chapter 6.

Invoice numbers can be a helpful way to track what you send out and what comes back, especially if you're sending many invoices to one outlet. Clients will use whatever invoice numbers you use, so feel free to make up a system that works for you and is easy to keep track of. It can be a combination of letters and numbers—once you develop a system, stick with it! As you can see in the example above, I created an alphanumeric system for each of the clients: Amp It Up Editing is AIU-2, AIU-3, AIU-4 ... LocalNews.site is LN-1, LN-2 ... this can help you keep track of how many invoices you have with each client, but even a simple numbered system will get the job done.

Aside from tracking your income, you will also want to create a spreadsheet **that tracks all of your business-related expenses** (see the example below). It's as simple as marking the date, what you bought, and the total cost—and a reminder to

	A	B	C
	Date	Item	Cost
1	2022-01-30	Monthly news subscription	$29.99
2	2022-02-21	Annual web hosting charge	$250.00
3	2022-02-28	Monthly news subscription	$29.99
4	2022-03-01	Annual Creative Cloud membership	$300.00
5	2022-03-02	Parking for Taco Battle reporting	$7.50
6	2022-03-10	Office supplies (notebooks, pens, batteries)	$35.50
7	2022-03-14	Printing costs	$15.25
8			
9	TOTAL EXPENSES		$668.23

still hold on to your receipts, too (which you can do physically or digitally). This sheet will help you keep an eye on what you're spending and will help you work more quickly come tax time. We'll talk more about what constitutes business expenses, also known as write-offs, in chapter 6.

If you're doing work where you bill hourly, I also suggest making a sheet that lets you **record all of your hours** in one place (see example below). Keep a column for the date, a short description of the work done, and the amount of time worked. You may find it easiest to keep a tab for each of your clients where you do hourly work, and to keep a running total at the end of each month to calculate what you will be invoicing. It's a document you can refer to if the client has any questions about your hours worked, and it will make things easier for you when you

	A	B	C
	Hourly work for Amp It Up Editing		
	Date	Description	Time (hours)
1	2022-06-05	Editing puppies promo	2.5
2	2022-06-10	Second-round edits	1
3	2022-06-14	Rendering and uploading files	1.5
4	2022-06-15	Editing kittens promo	2.5
5	2022-06-21	Second-round edits	1
6	2022-06-22	Meeting	1
7		Correspondence	.05
8			
9	JUNE TOTAL		10

invoice (which, in this case, would typically be at the end of every month). I also like to copy and paste the hours and work done to my monthly invoices, so clients have a clear idea of what the invoiced amount is for.

How to get paid

Ideally, you have already broached the question of pay with your producer, and you understand when and how you will be paid for your work. You've submitted everything to the outlet ... but when do you actually get paid?

This will vary depending on the client. Some will process the invoice quickly (our favorites!) and send along your check or your electronic transfer relatively quickly. Others wait a full 30 days (or longer) to release the funds. Many publications won't pay until the piece is printed—so if you know a feature story is a couple of months from release, you won't see that money for some time. And then, of course, there's the money that should have arrived but didn't come at all.

This is where your invoice spreadsheet comes in handy—make sure to update it when you send invoices out and when money comes in. Every once in a while, you'll want to check the spreadsheet for any invoices that haven't been paid in a reasonable time (say after a month, project-depending). That's when you will want to send a friendly follow-up email to your editor asking about the status of your payment.

In an ideal situation, the editor will get back to you quickly and the money is on its way. At the very least, you will hear when it should be on its way. But there are times, unfortunately, where you may not get a reply. You might follow up again, this time by phone. Nothing.

There are many freelancers who have been burned by an outlet—and other places known for not paying their freelancers in a timely way, if at all. Keep an eye on sites and message boards for the worst offenders, and avoid pitching to them. Your network of journalist friends can also help identify the places to avoid. If the outlet is a union shop, which isn't often the case, you might be able to seek support from the union. Otherwise, it's a matter of deciding how much effort it's worth to keep trying to get your paycheck.

With the growing number of freelance workers, more governments are stepping up to provide protection for contractors—though the response has been mixed. At the time of writing, two US states have passed laws with the intention of supporting contract and freelance workers: California and New Jersey. New York City also has legislation in place. If you live in one of these places, there may be alternate recourse if an employer has not paid you for your work.

When you get paid

When you get your first freelance paycheck—take a moment to celebrate! After a dance party, a selfie, and a few celebratory calls or texts, you make the deposit. But that isn't the end of the story. As you now well know—you *will* owe taxes on this income in the spring. The best way to avoid a surprise tax bill is to create a savings account and to set aside an approximate amount of what you'll owe at the end of the year. If your savings are a little under your total tax bill, at least you won't have to come up with a lot of money on short notice in April ... and if you save too much, you'll have the joy of a bit of extra cash in the bank!

To find out your approximate tax rate, look for tax calculators online for your state or province, or speak to an accountant or financial planner. An average amount to set aside is between 25 to 40 per cent per paycheck, depending on where you live. Thirty per cent is an ideal place to start. Some freelancers, like Erin Lowry from the Broke Millennial series, also choose to deduct their retirement or other savings at the same time as a way to ensure they're consistently putting money aside ... but right now, it's great if you're saving for a successful first tax filing.

And now, it's time to talk taxes. You may be dreading it, but you also knew it was coming, didn't you? In the next chapter, we break down everything you need to know about taxes as you start your freelance business.

Trevor Solway

filmmaker

When Trevor Solway graduated from Mount Royal University's journalism program in 2017, he already knew he wanted to work freelance. While still in school, Solway was working part-time as a videographer, making videos for clients and running film workshops and camps on his reserve, Siksika Nation.

"I had seen other people who were filmmakers or videographers who were already freelance and they were traveling and doing gigs and they seemed to be making it work. So I thought, I can make it work, too ... [And it] sparked the idea of filmmaking as a responsibility to your community as well, representing voices that aren't really heard in Canada," he says.

"Toward the end of my degree, I was getting impatient—I wanted to start making stuff full-time already. And I was just kind of envisioning this dream of making things full-time, making videos full-time."

Even though Solway had freelance experience, there were still a lot of things he had to figure out when he started on his own after graduation.

Photo credit: Trevor Wong

"They call it show business ... and I know a lot about the show, I don't really know a lot about the business side. Early on, I didn't really know how to do quotes or what to charge people, how to invoice, how to do my taxes, all that kind of stuff—I kind of just guessed along the way," he says. "I created a lot of problems for myself early on."

Solway learned the ropes as he went along. He used a starting rate he was given by another local filmmaker as his daily filming rate. After discovering that half-days of shooting generally became full days anyway, he stopped offering half-day rates. For editing, he charges by the hour. This is how he avoids scope creep in projects.

"Before, I would roughly quote for maybe $3,000 or $4,000, and then, once I would commit to that, my clients' ideas would grow out of control and we'd be interviewing this person, this person, this person. And the work would grow, but the budget wouldn't. Being young and naive, I would just go along with it," he says. "Now, I do meetings ... it takes a lot of consultation, and really mapping out and asking hard questions about this project. Who's going to be interviewed? Why and how long is it going to be? Where's this going to be shown?"

It's after a couple of meetings and firming up details on the project that Solway provides a quote—and a contract.

"[Earlier on] I wouldn't do contracts, but now, one thing I've noticed that keeps videos on track and in focus is a contract. And so I always refer to that when ideas get too big," he says. "I've been finding a pattern—if it's a five-minute video, it is probably 50 hours of editing. Ten minutes is probably closer to 100 hours or 80 hours."

When he was starting out, Solway recalls being told to say yes to every opportunity. "And so that's what I did ... And I over-committed myself and I would just be doing things that I wasn't really passionate about," he says. "I would work on like eight things at a time and all of them were corporate, events or promotional stuff. And one of them would be a passion project. This was probably for a year or two, and I wasn't really happy doing that."

It took him some time to gain the confidence to step out and take on his dream projects.

"When I started in 2017, I was just kind of grateful to be there and grateful for opportunities and a bit insecure. I think a lot of new grads kind of feel that," he says. "But I think about my mom when she was 29, she had an eight- and nine-year-old. She had to care for us, she had to work multiple jobs and she didn't get a chance to live out her dreams ... And so now, I kind of owe it to her and to my grandpa and everything they had to sacrifice for their kids, for me to be a filmmaker."

Now, Solway is transitioning from corporate video work to making films and television series. This has meant applying for grants—a skill that he began to develop back when he ran film camps for non-profits on his reserve.

"I think a lot of filmmakers, a lot of young writers and directors, they have all these big ideas. But when you just talk and talk and talk about them and don't take any action, they just kind of stay there in that talking stage," he says. "Grant writing is a part of lighting that match to get them started."

As he's learned, small grants lead to bigger grants and bigger projects. Solway's work is currently funded by the National Film Board, the Alberta Foundation for the Arts, and more. He's found that, instead of doing everything himself, working with a producer gives him the time and space to pursue what he loves most about filmmaking.

"Like I said, I'm not a business person. I'm not a money-oriented person ... when you just work on spreadsheets and you apply and navigate these grant portals, it's so soul draining," he says. "So now, I work with a producer, we work on these grants together. And so I get to write out the creative process and all that kind of stuff, but having someone just worry about [the details] is so great."

Eventually, Solway wants to be able to hire camera operators and editors so he can direct full-time. It's a far cry from being the shooter, director, and editor making videos for Siksika Nation, but he knows that he'll take what he's learned as he moves forward.

"Those videos sparked my interest in learning my language and learning the history. I'm grateful for the corporate videos I do back home because they teach me invaluable lessons of people who might not be here very much longer. It's not just a paycheck for me—it's bringing me closer to my community," he says.

"[But] every kind of story that I tell, if it's a passion project, whether it's a documentary or narrative film, it is inherently going to be an Indigenous film for my community, because it's coming from me."

Chapter 6:

Tax time

Taxes are often full of stress and complication, whether you work freelance or not. Being a freelancer means that your relationship with the government changes; you're no longer filing taxes as a citizen, but also as a business owner, and that affects how you pay your taxes. With a bit of research and planning, and some expert advice, tax time doesn't have to be scary—in fact, it can be liberating to have a better handle on your money and understand where it's going.

Most freelancers start out as **sole proprietors**, meaning that they are self-employed but not incorporated as a business. Simply put, this means that your business income is tied to your personal income, and you will file your taxes for your freelance work in the same filing as your annual personal income tax.

If you've worked as an employee, you'll know that your employer deducts tax from every paycheck. You may recall filling out paperwork at the start of the year, and from that information, your employer makes an estimate of how much tax you will

owe and holds a bit of every paycheck to pay the government at
tax time. This can be incredibly helpful, because it saves you the
effort of putting aside savings come April. It can also be a win
if you have tax credits (i.e., for tuition and books) that lower the
amount of tax you have to pay—if you have ever received a tax
return, you know how great it feels!

As a freelancer, you don't have an employer, which means
you don't have anyone to deduct tax from your paycheck. You
also don't have automatically deducted payments for government
plans or services, like unemployment insurance or federal retirement benefits. That means you need to have money set aside to
cover these additional costs.

"You're getting your full gross pay paid out to you," explains
Liz Schieck, a financial planner with the New School of Finance
in Toronto. "This is the bigger thing, on the tax planning side,
that gets people into trouble—not realizing really how much you
need to be in charge of saving for [your] own taxes. And setting
money aside every time you get paid so that you don't have this
great first year freelancing and then go to file your taxes and get
a whopping tax bill that you don't have the money for. That's sort
of the worst case scenario."

Schieck says that it's not the end of the world if you get hit
with a big tax bill, and that she's helped people bounce back from
the shock. But, with some planning, why not avoid the stress
altogether?

In her line of work, Schieck has met many clients who are
convinced that they are bad with money—but when she sits
down to talk with them, she finds that it simply isn't the case.
Being uncomfortable with money talk and actually being bad
with money are two very different things. And yes, while as journalists we often label ourselves as bad with math or statistics,
working with finances and taxes is really more about applying
specific concepts to our money than doing complex math. The
calculations are generally straightforward and, if you absolutely
can't be bothered to do it, you can hire your work out to a bookkeeper or an accountant. Before you label yourself as bad with

money, ask yourself *why* you think that's the case—your answer might be telling. All of this to say, keep an open mind for this chapter!

To figure out how much you will owe the government, you first need to know how much money you actually made in the year. That's why the core of tax preparation (or tax planning) is good bookkeeping: if you have a clear system for invoicing and are keeping track of the money coming in and where it came from, you're well on your way. As we discussed in chapter 5, having a system for writing, storing, and tracking your invoices and receipts is key to keeping track of how much money you're making and how much you're spending. It doesn't have to be complicated: you just have to know how much you've billed for, when, and what the work was. It can also help to keep track of when you received it, mostly so you can follow up if a check is missing. These are the records you'll be using when calculating your income tax.

It's also important to clarify that, while people often refer to "taxes" in the broad sense, there are different specific taxes you may or may not pay depending on where you live and the work you do. In this chapter, we're speaking specifically about taxes related to your income and freelance work.

In Canada, income tax is calculated and filed through the Canada Revenue Agency (CRA). While you submit everything once, you're actually filling out two sets of forms and paying two income taxes: one provincial and one federal. As a sole proprietor, you file your business income and expenses alongside your personal income.

In the United States, things are a bit more complex for sole proprietors. "There are two taxes at the federal level that you pay: income tax, [for] which you may or may not have an obligation, but there's also self-employment tax, equivalent of social security," explains Jonathan Medows, a CPA based in New York and founder of CPA for Freelancers. "In addition to the federal tax in the US, there are state taxes. Some states charge income tax, and then some cities or counties charge income tax as well, particularly in the Northeast and Midwest." If you're uncertain about what taxes you need to pay, check in with a professional or contact the Internal Revenue Service (IRS) to avoid any unpleasant surprises. It's also worth mentioning that, even though you file your taxes once a year, the government will most likely want you to prepay your tax liability, which means you will need to pay a quarter of your estimated taxes four times a year.

If you have incorporated as a business, or are looking to, your taxes will be completed differently, and we won't be covering those details in this book. That is definitely a situation where you want to speak to a qualified professional.

Making a plan

Tax planning sounds serious and complicated, but doesn't have to be. At its core, it's about understanding how much you make at your freelance job and how much you spend on reasonable costs to run your business. If you have a method of keeping track of both of these things, you'll be able to either calculate what you owe or hand it off to an accountant to do the calculations for you.

While you're probably thinking about all of the money you *don't* have to spend as you start your freelance career, especially on an accountant, Liz Schieck says it's worthwhile to book an appointment with a financial planner or an accountant to make sure you understand the ins and outs of what you need to keep track of—especially in your first year.

"When people don't feel like they have a plan, it's much more stressful. And I think what happens ... is that they just keep not starting. They know that they're supposed to be doing something. They know they're supposed to be setting aside for taxes," she says. "But the longer it goes, the scarier it gets and the more they avoid it—and that usually means the more expensive it's going to get the longer you wait."

Not only is the cost of these sessions a write-off (we'll get to those later in the chapter) but they can give you personalized advice on how much of your income you should be setting aside for taxes and what types of purchases and receipts you should be tracking for your business.

"The peace of mind is priceless," says Schieck. "But also, that money spent on getting the financial advice is going to be saved tenfold by your first year's taxes being ready. The moment when you file your taxes as a freelancer for the first time and have enough money to pay them all is well worth it."

Even if you decide you want to prepare and file your taxes on your own, paying for a one-on-one session with a professional can help you better understand the elements that go into filing your taxes properly. For what it's worth, I waited years before hiring an accountant and getting professional financial advice. While I understand that I was trying to save the money by doing it myself, I can see clearly now that my stress levels were higher and my returns generally smaller than had I sought out some professional support. While it may sound appealing to go it alone, the benefits of professional experience and advice can help you exponentially as you work through your first year (or few!) as a freelancer. If taxes and money planning stress you out, it's probably worth talking to a pro.

What's in a name?

A lot, when it comes to the world of financial planning! Here are a few terms to be aware of as you look to hire someone to help you with your finances:

Financial planners are professionals who require a mix of training and experience to earn their title and certification.

Financial advisors or advisers encompass a broader category of people working in the financial industry, which includes salespeople who are licensed to sell financial investments. In Canada, watch out for spelling—financial advis**e**rs have a fiduciary duty to their client, while financial advis**o**rs do not.

Fiduciary duty means a professional is legally obligated to act in their client's best interest. This is something you'll want to know upfront about anyone you choose to hire.

There are also different ways that financial professionals charge for their services, the two most common being:

Fee-for-service or **fee-only** providers will charge you by the hour or a flat rate for their time. They don't sell investments, and won't make any money off the choices you make based on their advice. You may also see the term **fee-based**, which may mean fee-for-service, but could also mean that the provider makes a small amount of commission from selling products. Be sure to clear up any definitions and find out any commissions before you hire someone.

Commission-based providers are paid based on the financial products you buy or the accounts you open—usually, a percentage of the sale. While some commission-based providers may have fiduciary duty to their clients, it isn't a requirement, so you will want to ask upfront. Most advisors at banks or brokerages are paid on commission.

Jonathan Medows, the founder of CPA for Freelancers, says that identifying when you need help—and hiring the right people to do the job—is part of a business mindset that will serve you well in your freelance career.

"People fail to realize that they're in charge of everything, everything that goes right, everything that goes wrong ... you're responsible. So you can't blame other people because ultimately you're going to pay the bill," he says. "So you can say, 'Oh, my bookkeeper messed up. She wasn't on top of it.' But you're writing the check, it's your responsibility, that won't mitigate it. You have to make sure that all of this stuff gets done."

This doesn't mean you have to be an expert in every part of business—but you'll want to be familiar and learn how to hire and interact with the professionals who can help you, whether they're accountants, lawyers, web designers, IT experts, or more.

"You have to be well-versed in different areas, or enough to have the conversation," says Medows. "So you have to be well read. Just as someone who goes to the liberal arts college should be well read in Shakespeare and in sociology and psychology ... when you run your own business, you should be up on the different spheres of business influence. And if not, if you don't want to handle it—and you want to be successful—perhaps running your own business is not for you."

Even though learning the ins and outs might seem tedious, understanding taxes and how you pay them isn't just about what you owe the government—it's about understanding your work and how to make a living doing it.

"I think that the most important thing is to know your business, know *where* you're spending your money, to know *why* you're spending your money," explains Tova Epp, a senior tax preparer for Artbooks in Toronto. "For me, being in control of how much money I owe or spend is important."

Looking to hire an accountant or business advisor? Here's Jonathan Medows's advice on what to ask a prospective hire:

1. Ask about their client base.

"Who are your clients? Who do you work with? Who's your ideal client?"

2. Explain your business situation.

"Do you have experience in this area? Do you have a couple of other clients you can give me as a reference?"

3. Are you licensed? Where did you go to school?

"Not that education is a be-all and end-all, but there is some validity to education and professional licenses."

4. Do you have insurance?
5. Confirm work deadlines, expectations, and fees.
6. Follow your gut.

"It's a combination of technical skills and interpersonal skills, because you can have a great person, but if it's not a good match, personally, it won't be good relationship. These are trusted advisors—you have to have a good rapport with them."

Make the government your friend ... or, at least, a friendly acquaintance

In her line of work, Tova Epp admits that she sees many clients who are scared of the CRA. She even had a client that paid her to come to his house to hold his hand while he called with an inquiry on his account.

"The government has so many Boogeyman qualities for so many people," she says. "So many of our clients have a trauma around the government; they can't call the government and they're afraid. And [it's OK] once they realize that, you know, we're paying tax dollars for somebody to sit there and answer the phone—and they're nice!"

These stresses can be fueled by very rational fears, like a looming tax bill. But, ultimately, the best way to keep tabs on your situation is by (occasionally) talking to the CRA or IRS. Since they are the department that approves your filings, they will usually be the best source of information regarding your taxes. And, as Epp pointed out, it is literally your tax dollars that hire the people that work in customer relations—so you have every right to take advantage!

"Learning to have a good relationship with the government is more imperative when you're freelance, because there's no buffer of having an employer do it for you," says Epp. "So developing a good relationship and good habits around your tax is really half the battle."

If you reach out to the government to ask questions early on, you can better plan your finances to be in good shape come tax time. And, if you're ever stuck with a big bill that you can't pay on time, a simple phone call can help you arrange a payment plan so that you aren't in default—which can save you lots of stress and extra fees. While calling the government with your tax queries is probably not on your list of top 10 activities, it is one of those chores that will help you save time and money in the long run.

"I'll just write it off!"

If you're a fan of the TV show "Schitt's Creek," you might remember a scene where David Rose (played by Dan Levy) is in his hotel room surrounded by all sorts of expensive items for a store he's managing. His father, Johnny Rose (played by Eugene Levy), walks in and asks him how he's paying for everything.

"It's a write-off," says David.

"That's a write-off? Do you even know what a write-off is?" asks Johnny incredulously.

"Uh, yeah," retorts David. "It's when you buy something for your business and the government pays you back for it."

"Oh? And who pays for it?"

"Nobody," sighs David in exasperation. "You write it off!"

If you're more of a "Seinfeld" person, there's a scene where Cosmo Kramer (played by Michael Richards) tries to explain to Jerry Seinfeld that breaking his stereo and making it look like a shipping accident is a write-off for the US Postal Service.

"Jerry, all these big companies, they write off everything," says Kramer.

"You don't even know what a write-off is," counters Seinfeld.

"Do you?"

"No, I don't!"

"But they do," says Kramer knowingly. "And they're the ones writing it off."

Needless to say, write-offs—and their implications on a business' bottom line—are often misinterpreted. While they can be beneficial to you and your business, they aren't as lucrative as some might have you think.

Write-offs are another way of saying business expenses, or the costs you incur while running your business. Let's say that, over the year, you spent $3,000 on items and services that you needed for your business. You kept all of your receipts and have some notes that you made about why these purchases were necessary.

By looking back at your invoices, you see that you made $10,000 in total freelance revenue that year. That means that, when filing your taxes, you can subtract the $3,000 in business expenses from your total freelance income. You will be taxed on a total income of $7,000 instead of the $10,000 you earned—which means the government is taxing you only on your **profit**.

But that doesn't mean you've made an extra $3,000—it just means you won't get taxed on the $3,000 you spent. If we assume a tax rate of 25 per cent:

$$\$10,000 \times 0.25 = \$2,500 \text{ taxes owing}$$
$$\$7,000 \times 0.25 = \$1,750 \text{ taxes owing}$$

Subtracting $1,750 from $2,500 means you've saved $750 in taxes—which is great! But you also spent $3,000 to save the $750—so in the long run, you still spent $2,250.

Liz Schieck says it doesn't mean you shouldn't be using write-offs—but it does mean you should keep in mind how they affect your bottom line.

"You will spend more money buying things to write off than you would paying your taxes. So you should still be mindful that you shouldn't just be buying things so that you can write them off. It has to be worth it to you," she says.

This means spending money on things you need for work, not simply buying for the sake of saving money on your taxes.

"The ultimate goal for any business owner is to be as efficient as possible in terms of keeping your expenses reasonable and as low as possible so that you maximize your profit, right? That's kind of what your business is all about ... otherwise, you're just spending money."

What counts as a write-off?

Now that you're familiar with the math around write-offs, let's talk about what actually counts as a write-off. When Artbooks' Tova Epp runs freelance tax workshops with students, she says it's always the #1 question.

"We usually do a dry erase board or a chalkboard and get people to brainstorm. And I say, 'What's a write-off?' No judgment. Just throw out what you think a write-off is," she explains. "And within the first five, pretty much always, is gym, dentist, rent, and food."

As you might guess, these examples aren't usually write-offs; these are costs you have regardless of whether you run a freelance business or not. When it comes to figuring out what to write off, you need to think about what you spend exclusively *because* of the work you do.

"So, for a journalist ... the tools you use to generate income, your writing, don't have a ton of write offs. There's not a lot of expense involved," explains Epp. "But if you were renting a studio outside of your home, if you had a hot desk somewhere, that's great. If you are paying for editor fees, if you're paying for mentoring classes, all of your online services that you're using for your computer [can be claimed]."

As Liz Schieck from the New School of Finance explains, what works as a write-off in some industries won't apply to others, so it's always best to talk to a professional or check the government's website for rules on write-offs.

"There are a ton of things that are absolutely a business expense for one person and absolutely not a business expense for another person," says Schieck. "And, also, lots of people write off things they shouldn't be writing off ... and you might not want to do that."

Many write-offs exist in gray areas and need to be considered from the business perspective.

"If you go to meet a client for lunch and you pay for your lunch, that was a business meeting. You can write that lunch off," explains Schieck. "So people go, 'Yeah, I can write off my meals!'"

But that doesn't mean that suddenly all meals can be written off. Let's say you happen to choose to work at a coffee shop one afternoon and ended up buying your lunch there.

"[Some may say] I was working, I chose today to work at this coffee shop all day, and I needed to eat because that's helping me get my work done, and that's helping me earn a profit in my business. So I can write that lunch off," says Schieck. "Well, those are two completely different things. You could have chosen to work at home that day. You could have chosen to pack a lunch. You could have chosen a number of things. Everybody has to eat lunch, even if they're an employee."

While meals and entertainment are a business expense category for write-offs, Schieck says they're often scrutinized because it's a place where the business and the personal overlap—and for that reason, you need to make sure you have the proper receipts and are claiming at appropriate times.

Tova Epp has a simple question for determining whether a cost should be considered as a write-off.

"We want to really focus on the ones that prove our intent to earn a profit because that's the government's criteria: What's your ability to show an attempt to earn a profit?" says Epp. "So I had a coffee with my writer friend, and that's a business expense. That's great. Probably was. You probably talked about business and ... how your writer friend's going to help you out later down the road. But if my business makes no money, that's not an expense."

That's because a write-off is what is "written off" from your total profit for the year. If, say, you make $10,000 in a year, you can only write off up to that $10,000—otherwise, your business is claiming a loss. That means that, if you're making a small amount of income at the start, you might want to strategize what you choose to write off.

"[As a business owner] I want to highlight the expenses that actually show I have an intent to earn a profit. So, advertising. If I have a website, great expense," explains Epp. "If I put up a show in a gallery and I have to pay for the opening night party, great expense, because I'm advertising my intent to turn a profit."

A year where you claim a loss might not be a problem, but Schieck says if you claim a loss several years in a row, you might hear from the government.

"Because you're writing off so many business expenses, there's a reasonable chance that the CRA might go, 'Are you sure you don't have a hobby? Because this seems like a hobby, not a business,'" she says. "And really, as far as most people are concerned, a business' point is to earn a profit. If you're not earning a profit because you're writing off so many things, do you really have a business? [It's about] being mindful of that and being reasonable."

You also have the ability to claim part of a receipt if only part of the cost is used for your business—cell phone plans, home internet, and running and maintaining your car are all examples of bills that you wouldn't write off in their entirety if you also have them for personal use. You could choose to write off half the cost, or a quarter of it, or a different percentage depending on how much of it is used for your business.

Another way partial claims might be helpful are if you travel for work—and decide to extend your stay. If you keep your receipts from your trip, and carefully keep track of what you were spending on your purchases, you can then later work out what expenses were work related, or partially work related, and plan to claim those come tax time.

Show! Me! The Receipts!

You have probably heard that receipts are important for taxes—and they are. Any expenses you claim as business write-offs need to be clearly marked with the date, the purchase, and the amount—and in Canada, they need to stay legible for seven years (the length of time the CRA can go back and audit you). In the

United States, the IRS recommends you keep documents for three years after filing, though certain paperwork should be kept for seven. When gathering your receipts and other paperwork, don't plan to use credit card statements—these aren't itemized receipts, which detail everything you bought and paid for. That's what the government prefers for tracking expenses.

Ideally, you should be keeping a copy of the itemized receipt and the receipt from the transaction—i.e., if you paid with a debit or credit card. But, especially in the digital world we live in, a digital itemized receipt should suffice for a write-off. If you aren't sure whether or not to keep a receipt, keep it—but make sure you write down for what the receipt is for.

"Make a note somewhere, whether it's on the receipt or in a spreadsheet or in some kind of bookkeeping software about what that expense was," says Liz Schieck. "Because in eight months you might not remember. That's good to have for your own records as well. Like, in five years, if the CRA asks you about it, you might not remember!"

However you choose to keep your receipts and make sense of them—analog, digital, or a mix of the two—Tova Epp says it's important to get in the habit of always asking for receipts.

"You have to ask for them all the time ... even though you're going to get a bunch you don't care about, you're going to have ones that you need," she says. "If you only ask for the ones that you need, you're going to forget."

As for a system, Epp keeps it simple—she has an open paper bag in her office where she regularly puts her receipts.

"For me, having a bag that's open and easily receives things just means that my receipts have an easy home," she explains. "When I come home, they just get dumped in there because it's accessible to me. And then, once a month or once a quarter, I can go through and put them into my accordion file, which is next door. But that bag is inviting. [It's about] making it as easy as possible."

Making your plan: Tracking expenses

1. How will you keep track of your physical receipts? Your digital ones?
   - it can be as simple as a bag or box to drop receipts (with small notes written about the expense), or you can digitize them to keep on your phone or on file.
2. How often will you go through and organize your receipts?
3. Where will you go to learn more about what constitutes a business expense?

Things that may count as business write-offs as a journalist

This isn't an exhaustive list, but a good start as you begin to consider and categorize what kinds of expenses might apply to your freelance work.

Your office space

Depending on your living and home-office situation, you can write off the costs associated with the physical space of your office. That is, if you own a home and use a room in the home for your work, you can write off a percentage of your mortgage interest, property taxes, and home bills (i.e., electricity) that align with the space the office takes up in your home. If you rent, you can write off a percentage of the rent that aligns with your office space along with a percentage of any utility costs.

Generally speaking, you need to be able to show that you have a dedicated space for your work, and it is your primary place of work for your freelancing. Simply put, you can't claim your dining room if it's where you do all of your work if it's also where you have dinner every night. Speak to a professional (or your accountant) to find out if your situation would allow for writing off your office space—and, even if it doesn't, you can still write off part of your internet costs and your cell phone plan as well as all of your physical office supplies—like pens, paper, a printer, etc.

Your gear

Depending on the work you're doing, you're in a position to write off the equipment you use exclusively for your freelance work, or write it off partially if you need it for work but also use it for personal use (like a laptop or your cell phone). This can apply to microphones or recording gear, cameras and accessories, like tripods, carrying cases, or SD cards.

For big equipment purchases that are designed to be used over several years, like a car, those are seen as capital costs, and you can't claim the full amount in a given year—it will be divided over the expected lifespan of the item (also known as an "asset"). Keep this in mind if you're looking to buy a big item with the expectation of a big return in the next tax year, as it won't necessarily all come at once.

Your car

If you bought a car for work use, this would count as a capital expense that you would write off over several years. If you leased a car for work use, you could write off the annual cost of the lease every year. The more likely scenario—if you already have a car, and use it for work and personal use, then you can keep track of your car costs and write off the percentage you use for work-related travel.

Ideally, you should be keeping a note of whenever (and wherever!) you drive for work, but that can be ... challenging. A simple way to keep track of your car use is to make a note of your odometer on January 1st and again on December 31st to see how many miles or kilometers you drove in the year. Keep track of all of your car-related costs: all gas receipts, all monthly insurance bills, all repair and maintenance appointments. You or your accountant will then be able to deduct the percentage of these costs based on how much you used the car for work (say, 25 per cent of the time means you will write off a quarter of your annual car cost). Don't forget any work-related parking costs, any roadside service plans you may pay for, and your annual costs for your license and registration.

Personally, I keep a tiny Moleskine notebook in my glove compartment to keep track of every time I gas up my car or take it in for maintenance—it takes only a minute or two to keep track and makes it much easier when it's time to calculate my car costs for the year.

Software and other monthly subscriptions

If you require a certain piece of software to do your work, you can write off its cost as a work expense. These days, you might be more likely to have a monthly subscription to a service—like Google Suite, Adobe Creative Cloud, Zoom, or online storage. With automated payments, it can be easy to forget you have these subscriptions, so scan your monthly credit card bill to make sure you include them all (while the statements themselves don't count as receipts, you should be able to find the receipts for these plans in your inbox or on your user account).

If you subscribe to any news outlets or magazines, remember to add those as well.

Meeting and entertainment costs

As discussed earlier in this chapter, this is a category that is generally heavily monitored when you file your taxes, because it can be a gray area. But that doesn't mean you can't keep your receipts—along with notes for the cost and why it was a business expense—which you can revise again at tax time. If you had a business lunch or dinner, hosted an event for your business or attended an event for work, you should hold on to your receipts to assess at year end if they're worth claiming.

Promotional costs

As a journalist, you probably aren't buying monthly billboard ads, but there are still promotional expenses: your website hosting and any web design fees, any professional photos or headshots, any accreditation costs or membership fees for professional organizations. If it's a cost that helps you gain business or establish your work, hold on to those receipts.

Work-related travel expenses

These claims can be as simple as a train ride to the next town over for an interview to plane fare and hotel costs as you travel to produce a documentary. In many cases, you may tack on some personal vacation to a work trip—and that's OK, you can still claim the parts of your travel that were related to work. Hold on to all of your receipts—and document what the costs were for—and you can make sense of all of it when you're back home (and have hopefully sold a really great piece of work!).

Moving costs

While not necessarily a freelance-related write-off, it's worth mentioning that, if you move a significant distance for a contract or permanent job—usually outside of your current city—you have the ability to write off your moving costs. This could include movers, storage lockers, mileage for the drive or plane fare, and a daily stipend for food during your moving days. If you do end up moving to take on a new work opportunity, it can be a way to save on your taxes for the year. This deduction is an option if you're filing your taxes in Canada; in the United States, the IRS eliminated the moving spending deduction in 2018, unless you're an active member of the Armed Forces. This is in effect until 2025.

But if I'm a business, shouldn't I incorporate?

You have likely heard of incorporation, which means legally registering your business as its own entity. It's a complicated process that should involve significant amounts of professional accounting guidance and legal advice.

Jonathan Medows says this is something that many of his new clients ask about. "The first thing they want to do is incorporate. I [try to talk] them out of it because they want to spend a lot of money from the get-go. And I'm like, 'Why don't you try it out and make sure you're successful?'" he says. "Because, if this is not viable, then these entities that you're setting up, you're going to have to shut down."

Thankfully, you don't need to incorporate to run a long and successful freelance career, and it certainly doesn't need be your first move as a freelancer. Take some time to see how much you earn in the average year, where your major business expenses are going, and whether freelance work is a long-term fit for you before even considering if it's necessary.

GST, HST, and sales taxes

If you're freelancing in Canada, you will likely need to consider registering for a GST or HST number before you consider incorporation. Simply put, when you begin earning more than $30,000 in a 12-month period from your freelance work, the government considers your income to be significant enough that taxes should be paid on your services. A GST or HST number, depending on your province, allows you to add the tax amount to your invoice and gather this tax amount from whoever you invoice for your freelance work. If you're thinking this is extra income for you, sadly it is not. You will owe this money to the government—basically, you become a tax collector for them.

There are some write-off benefits to having a GST or HST number, but there is also additional paperwork and filing deadlines, and as long as you're under the income threshold, there's likely no immediate need to file for a number. That said, keep an eye on your income and be ready to file for a number before your annual income hits $30,000, or you may end up owing back taxes—without having gathered the money from your clients, which could be costly for you. Also worth noting: this $30,000 is for any past 12-month period of work, not necessarily in a tax year.

If you already have an accountant, it is usually not significantly more expensive to have them file your additional GST or HST tax payments; an accountant or financial planner can also answer any questions around tax numbers and whether or not it makes sense for you to register.

If you're working in the United States, your freelance work may be subject to sales tax. The rules vary from state to state, so you will want to look into specifics for where you live and work. Jonathan Medows also points out that, depending on where you work, you may owe sales tax across multiple jurisdictions. "It used to be that you only had to collect sales tax in the state that you had a physical nexus, a physical presence there, like a warehouse there," he says. "And now this rule has changed so that, if you have economic nexus, i.e., you get a certain amount of sales in the state, you have to collect sales tax."

It's taxing ... but you can do it!

While all of the ins and outs of taxes may have your brain spinning a bit, taxes are actually quite simple in practice. Learn what rules apply to you and your work and, with research or the help of a professional, make a plan that fits your needs. Then it's about keeping track of the money that comes in and the expenses that go out. If you have a solid system of managing that, you can check in every few months or even once a year before tax time to assess what you have before sending it off to an accountant or filling out the paperwork yourself.

As your business grows or your work changes, there may be additional things to consider—like taking advantage of different write-offs. You may find yourself needing to apply for a GST or HST number, or you may decide it's worthwhile to incorporate. Remember that you don't need to know everything right from the start; as you become more comfortable working with invoices, tracking, and taxes, as you learn more terms and how they apply to your work, you'll gain a better understanding of the system and how to tackle any questions or issues that come up.

Kat Eschner

freelance science and business journalist

When Kat Eschner graduated with a masters in journalism from Toronto Metropolitan University in 2016, she knew she wanted to work freelance. After two intense years of study and a summer internship with the Globe and Mail, she needed a break from the busy newsroom culture.

Eschner was prepared for the journalistic work of freelancing, but the money side was a whole new challenge.

"Freelancing, running your own business in general, I think is a really great way to force you to confront every single anxiety and concern and misconception you have about money. And the process of untangling that, unfortunately, can take years just because money can be a very emotional thing," she says.

"We have a lot of ideas about how it should be made and how it should be spent—some of those we inherited maybe from our parents, some of those from society ... you have to sort out what actually matters to run your business in an effective way. And that's a real process."

For Eschner, that's meant learning how to navigate the tax system and begin planning her finances long-term. In her first

Photo credit: Britney Townsend

years of freelance, she chose to use software for her bookkeeping and hired an accountant to take care of her taxes.

"I didn't really realize when I started just how much overhead the administrative work is. It is actually a fair amount of work with a really huge learning curve," she says. "When I started my career I had that 'How can I possibly do taxes, because taxes are terrifying!' moment."

Like many freelancers, Eschner has many streams of income, from her part-time work as a contributing editor at Popular Science to her bylines with Fortune, the New York Times, the Guardian, and the Canadian Wildlife Federation's magazine, among others. This means she balances different currencies and payment schedules as she tracks her income, along with collecting HST from her clients with a Canadian tax presence.

Four years in, Eschner has decided to tackle taxes on her own this year—though still with the guidance of a relative who's a registered accountant. She continues to refine her workflow as she learns more about her business and what works best for her.

"Finding an organizational system that works for you is the core of freelancing ... We all live or die on how well organized we are," Eschner says. For her, this includes using apps for bookkeeping and tracking receipts, but going with a classic notebook for taking notes and running her daily schedule.

By balancing regular clients—like her work with Popular Science—Eschner has also been able to make sure that her set monthly costs are covered. "It's a baseline that means that I don't have to worry too much about paying rent, paying for the dog, for myself. It means that I can be a little more relaxed about when other payments come in or when I get other work."

Recently, Eschner has moved to a quarter system for her finances—planning for three months at a time instead of monthly.

"The stress of trying to make a certain amount every month led to short-term thinking about what assignments I would take [because] I would have to make my quota for this month ... So I'd take this $400 or $350 assignment to make my quota. But then doing that assignment took away from opportunities to do bigger stuff," she says. "So, when I transitioned into wanting to do bigger pieces, I started thinking quarterly."

As you navigate taxes and finances, Eschner's advice is to remember that it's OK if you don't know everything and making a mistake doesn't mean you're necessarily bad at freelancing. She remembers the stress of the first time she hadn't saved enough money for a tax bill.

"I was like, 'Oh my God, I'm such a bad person because I don't have the money and I didn't budget,'" she says. "I talked to other freelancers about this and they're like, 'We all hit this patch, open a line of credit—you don't want to use it, but it's better than maxing out your credit card.'"

For Eschner, it's a reminder that, while work and money are connected, the money you make doesn't determine your value as a person or as a journalist.

"Learning to decouple that from my feelings of personal worth was really a process, especially because freelancing is so much about your output ... You're not always going to have money if you're a freelancer, that's just the way it is."

Chapter 7:

Navigating the law as a freelancer

As journalists, we work within professional practice, journalistic ethics, and the law. Journalists who work at major outlets should be familiar with these laws and practices, but they also have access to ready advice. As freelancers without those supports, and with full responsibility for our own work, knowing the law is crucial.

What also complicates things is that, as students, you had certain internal supports when questions popped up—whether it was from professors in class or editors at student publications where you worked. You also had certain protections and rights for assignments that you produced for class, whether or not they were published. This means that, as a working freelancer, you may not be legally allowed to do certain things that were OK for a classroom assignment.

This chapter is meant to serve as a reminder of some of the overarching legal issues you should be considering as you pitch and produce your work as a freelancer in the field. It is certainly not a comprehensive list and should not be considered legal advice. I'll flag some resources at the end of the chapter if you're looking to continue your research.

Defamation

As you've likely learned in your media ethics or media law courses, there are many legal considerations that come with reporting on the stories and lives of others. Defamation, slander, and libel laws are made to protect individuals against untrue claims that can hurt their reputation or livelihood.

Simply put, defamation is the act of damaging someone's reputation. It can take the form of **slander**—a false spoken statement—or **libel**—a false written statement. If someone feels that you have hurt their reputation in a work that you have published, whether it's print, audio, or video, they can sue you for defamation.

While defamation laws exist to protect the individual, they only apply if the statements are false. That's why, as a journalist, it's important to use your strong reporting skills by corroborating facts from many sources and considering ethics when covering sensitive topics. There are many guides on media law and ethical practice for journalists, including guidelines from journalism associations wherever you're based. Seek them out if you're looking for more guidance on the legal and ethical implications of working as a journalist.

When you work as an employee for a media organization, they take on the responsibility for what is published and will usually have lawyers on hand to review stories that may tread into the territory of defamation. You may have heard of a story being "lawyered"—this means it's been reviewed and the wording is carefully edited to meet legal requirements (which means—don't change it without permission!). However, as a freelance journalist, this is something you are responsible for—though certain outlets will support the revision and fact-checking process before it's published. That said, most outlets these days will want to hold you responsible for any lawsuits that may come their way from a story you write. To better understand this, let's talk about liability and indemnity.

Liability, indemnity, and insurance

Liability (different from libel) is essentially responsibility for the work you're submitting—that you are responsible for the reporting you've done and the final produced work. But it isn't just the reporter who's liable for a story—the outlet that publishes it is liable, too. And that's why the outlet usually asks for **indemnity** from any issues that may happen with the story.

This is how Mike Anderson, a lawyer with Inter Alia Law in Toronto, explains indemnity: "Let's say you have a friend that's always late. You are both catching the same flight, and they ask for a ride. You say fine, I'll drive you to the airport, but if you make us late, you're on the hook for missed flight charges, hotel, and dinner. If your friend agrees, they are indemnifying you for costs they caused by being late. Basically, the concept is insulating yourself from certain risks, most often caused by someone else."

By indemnifying the outlet, you're agreeing to take on any of the risk that your story might cost—like being sued for defamation. These are terms that are usually determined by contracts you sign for your freelance work, and Anderson will have more advice for you on this in the next chapter.

So, if indemnity protects some from liability, then what recourse or solutions are there for the person who holds liability? This is where insurance comes in—you guessed it, liability insurance. If you're sued for your work, it can cover the associated costs.

To guarantee that you can actually pay out any damages (after all, freelancers aren't usually flush with cash!), some contracts will require that you have your own liability insurance. But liability insurance for journalists can be difficult to find and expensive to pay for, particularly when you're starting out.

For the most part, the freelancers I spoke to don't have liability insurance, citing cost and lack of options as main reasons for not being covered. They did, however, talk about the other ways they mitigate their liability in terms of the stories they pitch and how they go about their work—which can involve choosing less controversial stories, making sure your sources are credible and interviews documented, and corroborating information from multiple sources. Another option is to talk to your publishing outlet about having them cover you under their company insurance policy for the story.

Ultimately, in today's ever-growing (and increasingly litigious!) media landscape, liability insurance will likely become a bigger consideration for you if you plan to work mostly as a freelancer. Some groups that support freelancers, like the Freelancers Union in the US and the Canadian Freelance Guild, can provide support and information on available liability insurance for freelance journalists, and in some cases have special pricing for members.

Now that we've talked about some of the responsibilities you have as a freelance journalist, let's talk about some of the rights you have with your work—starting with copyright.

What is copyright?

Copyright is exactly what the name suggests: having the right to copy or publish something. Unlike trademarks or patents, you don't need to apply to own copyright to your work—if you produced it and it's original, your rights are inherent, and they begin as soon as your work is "fixed," meaning it is produced in some tangible way. In Canada, the Copyright Act governs copyright laws. In the United States, copyright is made up of many pieces of legislation but can be found in the Copyright Act, which is under Title 17 of the United States Code.

As a content producer, you hold the rights to your work. In Canadian copyright law, you hold **economic rights**—that you deserve compensation for others distributing or publishing your work. This includes the right to reproduce, publish, or perform an original artistic, literary, musical, or dramatic work. You also hold **moral rights**—protecting attribution and integrity— which means that you have a say when and how your work is used so that it's held in context and in line with your intent. As the creator of the work, you also have the ability to authorize or license your work as you see fit. In the United States, you hold economic rights only, but the rights are essentially the same—the right to reproduce your work, prepare derivative works based on your work, distribute copies of your work, and perform and display your work in-person and digitally. You also have the right to authorize or license rights to others, within certain limitations. In both countries, you don't need to use a copyright symbol (©) to protect your work, though it can be a helpful reminder to those enjoying your creations that you hold copyright.

Working as a freelance journalist, you are working with copyright from two sides. First, you hold copyright for the work you produce, and you can license or hand over copyright on what you make—which we will talk about more when we get to chapter 8. On the other hand, much of what we produce also involves using other peoples' work, so you need to be able to understand and respect their copyright.

Copyright applies to photographs, print music, film, digital media, podcasts, artwork, performances, and more. However, the *facts* and *information* you report as a journalist don't fall under copyright. If you were wondering how outlets can report facts and information based from competitors' reporting—that's why! But your overall article or final piece, how you "affix" your work, is. Currently, in Canada, copyright lasts for the author's life plus 50 years. But, starting in 2023, Canadian law will align with the United States and the United Kingdom, where copyright is the author's life plus 70 years.

You have likely heard about exemptions to copyright—and yes, there are ways that you can use copyrighted material in your work with permission from the copyright holder. As a student, you had copyright exemption for educational use. As a journalist, you have an exemption for the purpose of news reporting. But these exemptions aren't all-encompassing, and your work as a freelance journalist will come under more scrutiny than your work as a student, so it's important to know what your rights cover and what they don't. These rules fall under the fair dealing or fair use sections of copyright law, which we'll get to in a moment.

Even if you don't have an exemption to use copyrighted material, that doesn't mean you can't use it—it just means you need to reach out and get consent from the copyright holder. Later in the chapter, we'll talk a bit about how to go about getting consent for copyrighted work and the best way to document that consent in case copyright comes into question.

Fair dealing/Fair use

Both Canadian and American laws have a section that permits copyright exemptions for certain uses—in Canada, this is called fair dealing and in the United States it's called fair use. While there are some slight differences in their wording and application, both fair dealing and fair use provide protection for those using the copyrighted works of others for criticism, comment, news reporting, teaching, scholarship, and research. The goal of these exemptions is to promote freedom of speech, to encourage research, and to share information in the public interest.

But exemptions aren't just cut and dried based on the work you do; both American and Canadian copyright law have specific tests to help determine if the use of copyrighted work falls under the intended exemptions.

🍁 Fair dealing

In Canada, there are two tests to determine if your work falls under the exemption—first, you must look at the purpose of your work and determine if it falls under an allowable purpose as outlined in the Copyright Act. From there, there is a six-part test to determine if your use of the copyrighted material is fair:

1. The purpose of the dealing

What is your real purpose or motive in using the copyrighted material in your work? Does it serve the public good? For example, research or reporting for commercial reasons is less in line with the spirit of the law than, say, doing the same thing for charitable or educational purposes.

2. The character of the dealing

How is this information being shared, and with who else? Are many copies being distributed or just a few? Was the use of the copyrighted material reasonable to meet the project's outcome, or does it go beyond the scope of what was needed? If you destroyed the work after it was used for its intended purpose, that can also point to a fair use of the material.

3. The amount of the dealing

While you may sometimes hear people suggest rules such as "playing 30 seconds of a song is OK," the truth is there is no safe set use of copyrighted material. In some cases, i.e., a photograph, there isn't exactly the option of using only part of the work! Instead, consider the context of your project and ask yourself how much is truly needed to meet the goals of the fair dealing use.

The amount of the work you use isn't the only determinant of fairness, but it can help in the decision. Is it possible to use part of the work and still meet the goal, like in an article review? If you used the whole work, why is that necessary? This is considered alongside the purpose of your own work and its importance in terms of public good.

4. Alternatives to the dealing

This question asks: Was there a way you could have completed your work without using the copyrighted material? For example, if writing a review of a book, do you need to include passages of the book to make your point? Did you really need to use that Elvis track as a theme song for your podcast? In these cases, the courts would look to whether there were reasonable alternatives, such as using non-copyrighted equivalents.

5. The nature of the work

Is your project or work published? Unpublished? How many people will access it and how? In this case, if the work is confidential, or shared only among a small group of people, it suggests that you're using copyrighted material for personal benefit rather than public good, which might suggest that the dealing is unfair.

6. Effect of the dealing on the work

This asks how this new work affects the existing copyrighted material. If, for example, your reproduced work now competes with the market of the original material, that's a sign you aren't dealing fairly in your use.

As you can see from these two tests, journalistic work generally falls under the scope of fair dealing. That said, under the Copyright Act, **you are still required to cite the source in your work**, along with the name of the author, performer, maker, or broadcaster.

★ Fair use

In the United States, the test is very similar, though the determination of fair use considers four questions:

1. Purpose and character of the use, including whether the use is of a commercial nature or for non-profit educational purposes

Again, how you use the work makes a big difference. While non-commercial or educational uses are more likely to be considered fair, it isn't guaranteed. The court will look at the balance and purpose of the use—and if a work is transformative, meaning it is significantly changed from the material it referenced and doesn't act as a substitute for the original work—it is more likely to be considered fair.

2. Nature of the copyrighted work

This looks at the Copyright Act's goal of encouraging creative expression. Remember, facts and ideas aren't copyrighted, but the way they are affixed is. So if you're referencing more creative works, like a book, movie, or song, it's more likely to be considered unfair than referencing factual works—like a technical article or news story.

3. Amount and substantiality of the portion used in relation to the copyrighted work as a whole

How much of the work did you actually use? It might seem like using less work is more fair than using a big piece, but it also depends on the context of the work and the part you reference. In some circumstances, you might have to use the whole work—i.e., a photograph—and that can be considered fair. However, if you reference a small part of a work that is essentially the heart of the piece, the court could still consider it unfair use.

4. Effect of the use upon the potential market for or value of the copyrighted work

This is where the court looks at how your use of the work affects the copyright holder. Does it harm the existing or future market for the work? For example, if your use of the material is displacing sales of the original, that's a sign of unfair use.

If you're interested in learning more about US court decisions related to fair use cases, the US Copyright Office maintains a Fair Use Index where you can review past cases and court decisions.

It's important to note that fair dealing and fair use are defenses for using someone else's copyrighted material, *but it doesn't actually stop someone from suing you if they feel you've misused their work.* Since fair use and fair dealing are assessed on a sliding scale of "more fair" to "less fair," you might find yourself wanting to get additional clearances or permissions ahead of time if you're concerned that the owner may choose to pursue legal action—just to avoid the extra time, stress, and money that would come with it.

Clearing copyrighted work

While the news reporting exemption under fair dealing or fair use covers a lot of ground, it doesn't mean that all of your work as a journalist will allow you to use copyrighted material. For example, if you're creating content marketing for a company, that article is for a commercial purpose. If you wanted to produce a podcast about local news and events, the clips and discussion are likely considered reporting, but the other audio assets, like theme songs or sound effects, aren't.

If you want to use copyrighted material but aren't covered under the exemption, it doesn't mean you can't use copyrighted material—it just means you need to get clearance to use it. In short, you need to ask for permission from the copyright holder.

Getting clearance

While the idea of getting clearance or negotiating copyright might seem daunting, it's not that complicated. Much like reaching out to a potential source for an interview, getting clearance means getting in touch with the copyright holder to explain how you plan to use their content. From there, you will negotiate the terms of how you use their work, how the creator will be credited, and if or how you will compensate the copyright holder for the license.

While much of your journalistic practice has been based on verbal permissions or another type of informal agreement, you will want to have this agreement in writing. Emails may work in certain situations, but a more formalized document will serve you better in case of a disagreement down the line. The document should clearly outline *what* from the copyrighted content you will be using and *how* it will be used, including any places the work might be published. You will also want to clarify that the copyright holder has no rights to approve or edit your work prior to publication, which means that they won't get a chance to see your final work before publication.

Usually, this will first involve tracking down whoever made the content you want to use. If a photographer is clearly credited for a photo, that is where you would start if looking for permission. Some things on the internet might be a bit trickier—say, a video associated with a YouTube account but no author name. In this case, you'll need to likely message the account and use your research skills to dig a bit deeper on other ways to reach the author.

It's important to note that content creators, while they originally hold copyright, may no longer hold those rights or may have licensed them to a specific publisher or company. For example, if you're wanting to reference or quote a section from a book, the author may still hold copyright—but there's a good possibility that the rights have been signed over to the publisher. In this case, you can reach out to both the author and the publisher to determine who grants permissions. Another example where authors typically don't hold copyright to their work is music—it has usually been signed off to both the record label, who owns the recording rights, and the publisher, who represents the songwriter. This means that you will need two approvals for the rights to a song, likely without ever speaking to the person who wrote it. In the case of licensing music, expect to pay a fee for use.

Even if you have clearance to use a copyrighted work because of your journalistic exemption, you still might want to reach out to the copyright holder and ask for permission. Aside from avoiding the stress and extra work that might come with the owner accusing you of copyright infringement, you may also get access to a key source for your story. Sure, you could just grab a photo of a tornado tearing through downtown off Twitter—but talking to the person who posted it might be able to give you an exclusive in-person account for your piece. Perhaps you want to get additional context or information from the creator, even if you already have the right to use under fair use or fair dealing. On the other hand, if you have rights to use the photo and the source says they don't want you to use it, you might find yourself in an ethical quagmire as to whether or not to actually use the work. Use your judgment as to when and how you seek approvals.

So who actually enforces copyright law?

Copyright law is usually enforced by the owner—that means that if they saw someone misusing their copyright, they have the right to reach out to whoever is violating copyright and demand action, often in terms of payment or removing the copyrighted material if possible. While some copyright holders have companies, lawyers, or individuals keeping an eye on the use of their materials, that is typically not the case for smaller scale copyright holders.

So, while copyright exists, it is entirely possible to use copyrighted material and never hear from the owner. It depends on the nature of the content and how invested the owner is in protecting their copyright. As you might guess, you are more likely to receive a cease and desist letter from the Walt Disney Company than you are from an independent artist. But just because you might get away with something doesn't mean you should—and if you are planning to sell your work to an outlet or publication, you absolutely need to have clearance before it goes live.

This also means that you are responsible for enforcing your own copyright—or hiring someone to do it for you. How you go about enforcing will likely depend on the nature of the work, your intention for using it in the future, and how it has been used. If, for example, you produce work for a client and assign your copyright to them in your contract, then the person you have sold it to will now enforce the work—and they are entitled to any income that might come from any legal settlements around enforcing copyright.

If you do discover an egregious use of your copyrighted work and want to pursue it, there are many legal clinics that can provide you with guidance on how to proceed. In the simplest scenario, you contact the person using your copyright and they agree to take down or pay you for licensing; in the most complicated, you will be suing a person or a company.

Registering your copyright

As we talked about earlier in the chapter, you hold copyright as soon as your work is fixed; you don't need to register your copyright to hold it. In both Canada and the United States, however, you do have the ability to register your copyright with the Canadian Intellectual Property Office (CIPO) or the US Copyright Office. Unlike registering a patent or a trademark, the office doesn't investigate and confirm your copyright; they issue a certificate confirming your registration and your copyright claim is filed in a national database (for the US Copyright Office, see https://www.copyright.gov/; for CIPO, see https://www.ic.gc.ca/ eic/site/cipointernet-internetopic.nsf/eng/h_wr00003.html).

A copyright certificate can be helpful in that it provides a constructive or public notice of your copyright. It can be used in court as your claim to and enforcement of your copyright but, because the contents of your registration aren't verified by the offices, the certificate—and your copyright—can still be challenged. In certain courts in the United States, you have to register your copyright in order to be awarded statutory damages.

Copyright registration is provided for individual works—for example, if you wanted to register a newsletter or podcast you produce, you would need to register each episode individually. Those fees would add up! Realistically, registration is not required for everything you produce, and might be something you never do as a freelancer. But some big projects or creations might warrant registration—and in the case of transferring copyright to another holder, they may want to have the transfer registered to confirm their copyright.

While copyright might sound like a complicated concept—and to be fair, there are many scenarios where it can get more complex—it really comes down to understanding who owns work, finding a way to give credit, and using your research and interview skills to find the right people to get any necessary clearances. It's also about understanding copyright so you can enforce your own when needed, particularly in contract negotiations if an outlet or a client is looking to own rights to your work. We'll tackle that discussion in the next chapter.

Rebecca Collard

broadcast journalist and writer

Rebecca Collard's introduction to news writing was in a first-year course at the University of Victoria—and she loved it so much, she decided to pursue a minor in journalism along with her degree in political science. But it was a nine-month internship with the Terrace Standard, a community paper in northwestern British Columbia, that was her first time working in the field.

"It was an amazing experience," she says. "It was really fast, you know, baptism by fire into journalism, because all I had done before was stuff for my classes."

One of the highlights for Collard was traveling to Nisga'a Territory to report on elections after the Nisga'a Treaty—the province's first modern land treaty—came into effect in 2000.

After an internship with the Canadian International Development Agency (CIDA) in Ottawa, Collard knew she wanted to travel internationally. She took jobs with non-government organizations (NGOs) in Nazareth and Morocco, but something was missing.

"I learned so many things, but I felt kind of removed from what I wanted to be doing," she says. "I'd rather be, you know, writing about what NGOs are doing with a critical lens."

Through a friend, Collard found out that Egypt Today, a small English-language magazine, was hiring. She took the job and used the work and the steady salary to set up a home base in Cairo.

"It is a really great way to kind of have a soft landing—to find a local English language publication. And even if you're going to work there mostly as an editor, or you're going to get to write some articles, it means that you don't show up in a country with no support network, no income," explains Collard. "It also gave me a year to really understand Egypt a lot better and to make connections and networks and understand what was going on."

A year in, Collard felt confident enough to quit her job and start freelancing—first with better-paying regional English language publications and then moving up to bigger outlets. Today, she's based in Beirut and regularly reports on the Middle East for the CBC, Foreign Policy, Public Radio International, and more.

"The thing that I love about journalism is experiencing the world in this incredible way," she says. "Sometimes it's showing my Lebanese friends parts of their city that they don't know about because, as a journalist, you go to places that you wouldn't normally go, you get out of your bubble."

But the work comes with its challenges, too. Much of Collard's work is news reporting, which means her days are driven by what happens in the region—and meeting outlets' reporting deadlines.

"I might think that I have a plan for a day ... like I might think that today I'm going to finish this radio package, this feature package that I was working on. And instead it turns out there's a bombing in Syria and [that's] my whole day."

While breaking news runs the schedule of many reporters, working freelance means you're always on-call—especially with dwindling numbers of outlets funding their own foreign correspondents. Turning down work can be difficult when you're looking to maintain relationships and aren't sure when the next job will come.

Collard's favorite days are when she's in the field, and she's had the opportunity to report on the front lines all around the Middle

East. However, as a freelance journalist, this also means that she's responsible for her equipment, her insurance, and her safety.

"A big thing about being a freelancer overseas, that you think about all the time, is about risk versus reward," she says. "I mean, we've seen so many freelancers in the last 10 years, especially in Syria, who have been kidnapped or killed ... I don't want to say because they were taking risks that they shouldn't have been taking, but sometimes that's it."

For Collard, research and planning help her assess an environment and how she approaches her reporting. This includes checking in with contacts in communities to understand the risks before traveling, and hiring reliable and experienced fixers to help navigate in the field.

"Your safety is the most important. And if you take a risk and get yourself injured or killed, you're not going to be able to tell the story. So it's really not worth it," she says. "We've all seen what the 'bang-bang' looks like—is it really important that you see it?"

By looking away from the immediate action, Collard finds she's able to tell the stories that others might be missing—while also maintaining her safety.

"I feel like I'm relatively cautious ... When you're going to take a risk, how important is that risk compared to the story—is the story even important? Why are you running toward the front line?"

Chapter 8:

Contracts and negotiations

Why contracts?

Freelance agreements can range from handshake deals to multi-page written contracts. While many freelancers will accept handshake deals or informal agreements via email (and I will admit that this formed the bulk of my freelance work, especially when starting out!) it's important to be able to use, understand, and negotiate contracts as a freelancer. While formalized contracts might seem intimidating, there are lots of benefits that come with understanding how to use one.

"I always encourage freelancers to secure their deals by contract—that could be based on their own template, or a template provided by the folks hiring them," says Mike Anderson, a lawyer with Inter Alia Law and founder of Lagom, a legal platform for creative freelancers. "Developing your own template helps you think through your own service offering. It can also help you avoid awful situations like clients refusing to pay or using your intellectual property without permission."

A contract doesn't have to be 20 pages of legalese. According to Anderson, who works with many freelancers in the creative field, even a three-to-five page agreement can go a long way to outline expectations and provide a more defined working situation than a handshake deal.

Depending on where you freelance, contracts may be drafted up by the client as part of any project or work they hire for. In this case, you'll want to learn what clauses to look out for and how to go about negotiating any changes. But if you find yourself working with clients who often don't have written contracts ready, it might be helpful to develop your own template for **an independent contractor agreement** (the term for a contract between a freelancer and a client). You can use something you find online, or hire a lawyer to draft up a template for you, so that you can provide your own contracts. We'll get to both later in the chapter, but first let's go through some definitions and concepts that will help you make sense of a contract.

Elements of a contract

Here are some terms that you might encounter when reviewing or writing up a contract:

Scope of work

Your contract should explain the work you will deliver, and the deadlines it should be delivered by. While you might think delivering an article is straightforward—and it might be!—this is also where any additional expectations are listed, such as accompanying photos, audio, or video; social media posts or promotion; or other assets.

It is also a good idea, depending on the client or the work, to determine the number of revisions that will be included in the scope of work and when they will happen. In some types of work, i.e., quicker turnaround with daily newspapers, you likely have an idea of the editing timelines and expectations. But when you move into writing a feature piece for an online outlet, or perhaps writing copy for a website, you may find that what you think are reasonable amounts of edits and what your client thinks is reasonable are vastly different. This is sometimes called "scope creep"—when you find that multiple small asks from a client make the job much bigger than you expected or agreed to.

This is an area where Anderson thinks contracts can be hugely helpful—by clearly stating what you will deliver, when, and how, it's easier for both parties to be on the same page, with no surprises later. If everything is clearly laid out, it's easy to point out what is or isn't within the scope of work. For work outside of the scope, you can provide a list of additional services and their all-in cost, or assign an hourly rate for your work and negotiate with your client when and how to bill the additional amounts.

Pay

Since pay is a good part of why you're completing this work, you'll want to confirm how much you're getting paid for this project. But it isn't just about how much you'll be paid—as someone who works in a field of inconsistent paychecks, you want to look at *when* and *how* you'll be paid.

"For example, it's super important for a freelancer to get paid within a certain period of time, to get upfront payment or partial upfront payment whenever possible," explains Anderson. "It's really hard for freelancers to get paid *after* they have fully delivered their services, so I always recommend that freelancers are at least partially paid before they deliver everything."

Having at least some part of your payment up front is ideal, especially for a longer-term project. That said, many outlets have a policy of not paying until your work is published—but it's worth seeing if an early installment is possible. If you're doing less traditional journalism work, it may be easier to negotiate.

"The structure can always be customized," says Anderson. "The ideal is getting paid in full upfront, which can be hard to get. If this isn't possible, freelancers should negotiate for a deposit, and then regular installments based on a set schedule that lets you withhold services if payments don't arrive on time."

Anderson also recommends setting payments to specific dates instead of work delivery, if possible. Imagine you were able to negotiate an early installment that was to be sent after your client revises the first draft—but then you're stuck waiting on revisions for payment. By setting a specific date, you know money will be coming even if you're waiting on client feedback.

Rights

Ultimately, this comes down to who owns the content being published. Many freelancers are saying they're seeing more and more contracts that expect the journalist to hand over all rights to the story—for all future media formats and use.

If you're writing a small brief for a newspaper or online newsletter on a topic that has been assigned to you, owning the rights to what's being published might not be that important. But for bigger projects, original stories that you develop and pitch, you might want to take these beyond the original freelance piece. Maybe you want to turn it into a book, or a podcast series—and to be able to do that, you need to hold on to the rights to your story.

This is where it's important for a contract to denote **ownership** versus **licensing**. Ownership means you own the content and can do what you want with it. Licensing is when the content owner decides to let certain outlets publish their work, usually with some form of exclusivity. After all, what value is your content if anywhere else can publish it, as well?

When you can—"Keep your ownership, but license your right," suggests Anderson. He adds that licenses can be limited by time and jurisdiction if it makes sense to include these elements in your agreement. You can also divide your copyright and licensing for different media platforms or to include different elements of a piece: e.g., written story, accompanying photos or videos.

"There are many ways to do it, and just think about it rationally. What is this being printed in? So my license is for my story to be printed in this thing. And this edition, can it live on their website as well? Can it live in these other places and be really clear with what you're licensing in general?"

Some major outlets ask for you to sign over the rights whenever you publish with them. You will also want to watch out for "work for hire" or "work made for hire" language, which is a US term that means your work will be owned by the company who's paying you. In the case where the work is very much aimed at the company and you don't have any real use for the ideas and content outside of the contract, this may be fine to sign away ... but if this is the start of something bigger that you want to pursue in your freelance career, signing away your rights could stop you from developing and benefiting from those ideas in the long run.

"If I was a freelance journalist with a great story idea, I would fight to maintain my right to develop—or sell—that story for a podcast series, book, film, or other work. The most important part of that fight would be turning down any clause that seeks a full assignment of rights," says Anderson. "These are intangibles that we're working with ... And protecting your intangible property is super important."

Liability, indemnity, and insurance

While in many contracts you will see that the outlet wants rights to your story, you might also see that they want you to hold **liability** for your work and **indemnify** them from any issues that might come out of your work.

Since writers and publishers are liable for what is published, it means that by indemnifying the outlet, you as the reporter agree to take on all of the risk that your story might cost—like being sued.

"It always depends on what the indemnities call out, but a normal agreement in this instance about content is, 'Hey, you made this content; if we're sued because of your work, all liability flows to you and we won't be out of pocket for your mistake or bad work,'" explains Anderson.

Anderson says to keep an eye out in the indemnity section of a contract that says "you indemnify us for a breach of your representations or warranties or a breach of the agreement in general."

"When it comes to the breach of the agreement, if you're outside of the black and white letters of the agreement, then you will be responsible for any claims, costs, and damages that flow from that breach."

That can include anything from a missed deadline costing the client money to the client being sued for the use of copyrighted material.

"For the freelancer, it would be preferable to indemnify only for breach of representations and warranties, especially if that list is kept small," explains Anderson.

The idea of a reporter being held liable for what you report isn't entirely unreasonable, as you are the one making sure you follow proper practice and guidelines as you write your story. But what about the content you don't add to your piece—edits made in vetting that are inaccurate, or adding music, clips, or other elements after the fact? This is where Anderson suggests that you put this responsibility back on the client, clarifying that they will be held liable for any requirements, additions, or edits that they make.

Most contracts will require that you have your own liability insurance. But finding affordable liability insurance for journalists can be difficult to find and expensive to pay for, particularly when you're starting out. On the other hand, now, who does have liability insurance? The outlet. It can be worth asking them if you can be covered by the company insurance policy while you complete your assignment.

"That doesn't necessarily cost your client extra money," explains Anderson. "So if you're worried about risk, add one line saying that you will be added as an insured to their commercial general liability insurance, professional liability, or media liability insurance, and ask for proof that this has occurred."

Negotiating a pre-existing contract

If you're working with a large, established outlet, you will likely be handed a boilerplate contract, meaning it's a standard template given to all freelancers. You might think this means everything is set in stone; it isn't. But there are certain parts of the contract that will likely be more negotiable than others. An independent contractor agreement is usually made up of **business terms** and **legal terms**. The business terms tend to focus on the deliverables, deadlines, and payments, while the legal terms focus on rights, liabilities, and indemnities.

"The person you're working with is often not the lawyer, so they might have the ability to negotiate business terms," explains Anderson. "But then when it gets into the harder [aspects], like legal terms, indemnities, representations, and warranties and things like that, they often don't have authority to change that stuff. And if you insist on it, then it has to go to the legal department, and that means it can take weeks or months to actually finalize. This could be a problem if either side has a strict deadline to meet."

While you will likely have more success negotiating deadlines, deliverables, and compensation, all you can do is ask and see what happens. But the best negotiators plan ahead—so let's go over techniques that can help you in negotiations. While we're discussing this in the context of contracts, these concepts apply equally to negotiating pay, scope of work, and more.

Preparing to negotiate

Negotiation is about two parties coming together to a middle ground agreement—rarely, if ever, would you see one party getting their way entirely. That's why, when preparing to negotiate, you need to think about what options work for you outside of your ideal scenario.

You may have come across the acronym BATNA—in the negotiation world, it stands for **best alternative to a negotiated agreement.** As it implies, you'll want to know what you need from the agreement before you even begin negotiation.

Even if all of this is new to you, as a journalist you have developed one particularly helpful skill for negotiation—and Mike Anderson says to take advantage of it.

"I would say probably journalists would be more skilled in negotiation because they're used to hard conversations," notes Anderson. "That said, there are some differences between negotiating a contract and pushing for answers on a tough question."

There are ways to get comfortable with negotiation. The first thing to acknowledge, according to Anderson, is that negotiation can be more of a game than you may expect.

"In an ideal world, you could just say, 'Here is a fair agreement that I'm willing to accept.' And the other side says, 'Great! I think that's fair. Let's sign on the dotted line and get lunch, friend!'" he says.

"But this just isn't how things work, unfortunately. In negotiations, it's usually the person who pushes the hardest that wins. This sort of dynamic can feel weird. If you can accept this at the beginning, then you might be able to advocate your position more comfortably."

When negotiating, it's important to keep the following in mind:

Stay calm

Though you might feel stressed or flustered, preparing ahead of time can help keep you calm in your discussion. Focus on your goals and remember that none of this discussion is personal.

Use an approach authentic to you

You may have a view of what a "negotiator" looks like—but just like there are many styles of effective interviewing, there are endless ways you can negotiate successfully.

"If you are a funny person, you can use your humor. If you're a quiet person, you can use silence to be really powerful," says Anderson. "If you are talkative and persuasive, obviously that's useful, but there are different approaches."

Determine your anchors

Anchors are facts, figures, or examples that add weight to your argument. For example, if you're asking for more money on a project, you might make sure you have data for the average cost of that service in the industry.

"It's harder for somebody to undercut you when you're talking about an industry norm, or you're talking about something you were paid for last time, or you're talking about something you've been paid for 20 times in a similar way," says Anderson.

Anchors aren't that different from when you use facts and figures to back up arguments or statements in your reporting—use this skill to dig up compelling and authoritative examples that will support your case as you make your ask.

Determine best-case scenario

Before stepping into a negotiation, it's important to think about what you want from the agreement. Think of this as a checklist of your ideal situation: How much would you be paid? What would the deliverables be? When are the deadlines? Who owns the rights?

Some of these elements might seem basic to write down, but having them in front of you will make it easier to quickly assess what the other party's offering.

Determine best alternative

In case you can't negotiate terms that satisfy your best-case scenario, you should be ready to lean on alternatives available to you. Once you've decided what your alternatives are, you can determine (and leverage!) the point at which you would walk away from the negotiation.

"This is also very powerful," says Anderson. "Let's say you are offered $5,000 for a project. If you know that you can secure a similar deal for more than that, it's easy to ask for higher pay. And if they don't budge, you will be ready to say, 'Okay, well then this isn't for me; I have a better opportunity.'"

In short, setting up your limits ahead of time means you're less likely to accept a deal that you might regret later on.

Bridging the gap by adding value

If the other side isn't meeting your best alternative, it doesn't mean you need to walk just yet—Anderson suggests seeing where you can add value to bridge the gap between your offers.

"A great thing to say is, 'Okay, so if it's not X (amount of money) that you're looking for, how can we find a way to solve this problem? What else are you interested in? How can I increase the value?'"

As you're preparing for your negotiation, Anderson suggests listing additional things you can offer to sweeten the deal—ideally, things that offer additional value to the client without taking too much time or effort on your end. For example, let's say you and your client have a gap on the rate of pay. Perhaps you're open to accepting a lower rate of pay if you're paid entirely upfront for the work. Or, for your proposed rate, you can agree to license additional rights to your work—e.g., additional photo use for advertising and social media—particularly if the work is something you wouldn't be able to sell elsewhere. Then you get your ideal compensation, and your client has additional work they can use.

Ultimately, this type of collaboration requires good will and creativity from both sides, and that's why Anderson always recommends the following:

Email is not your friend

As much as you might dread doing it, these collaborative conversations work better in real-time.

"I think that, by far, better results are achieved by phone, in person, or even by video conference," says Anderson. "There are some things that you can do by email, but that greater conversation about hidden value, for example, never happens there."

Aside from developing connections and being able to determine where wiggle room might be in the contract, speaking in real time can also help you keep good a relationship with the other side. After all ... it's quicker to send off a short email, but those messages can very often (and easily!) come off as thoughtless or even mean.

"There's stuff that's more black and white that you can finalize, if you've been back and forth on fees, sure—maybe you can finalize that over email. But in general, I don't think you're going to get better results over email," he says.

How to build your own independent contractor agreement

Depending on your freelance situation, you may decide to draft up your own boilerplate contract for working with clients. While you can find many templates on the internet, Anderson recommends that you hire a lawyer to draft up your documentation—not only does it ensure that the language is appropriate for your jurisdiction, it's also an opportunity to go over the contract with a professional so you can feel confident adjusting it to specific projects and clients down the line.

You can hire a lawyer on a limited scope retainer, which means for a specific project only. Anderson suggests asking for recommendations when seeking a lawyer, and taking advantage of a free consult to explain what you're looking for. You don't have to go with the first lawyer you speak to!

Much like how you work with a client, the same will apply once you decide to hire a lawyer. Just like you would have a scope of work outlined for when you work for a client, you will want to do the same. The lawyer should be able to provide a quote for the work and you can agree on when and how they will be paid. If you're concerned about cost overruns, you can also set a cap for the fees—the max amount the lawyer can bill before coming back to you. This will all be drafted into the engagement letter that the lawyer will provide that confirms your agreement.

While the cost for this work varies by lawyer and by region, there are advantages to being able to work quickly and comfortably with a contract you understand. "If you're really confident in your paper, in the template you have, it means you'll move faster. It means you'll get a better deal and a deal that truly suits your specific needs," says Anderson.

If you're looking for more on how to negotiate ...

Arguably, *Getting to Yes: Negotiating Agreement Without Giving In* by Roger Fisher, William L. Ury, and Bruce Patton (1981, with updates in 1991 and 2011) is the foundational book on negotiation—it literally coined the term "win-win negotiation"! But there are lots of books, podcasts, and articles dedicated to the art of negotiation, if you want to take a deeper look at techniques. *Getting More: How You Can Negotiate to Succeed in Work and Life* by Stuart Diamond (2012) is a book that challenges a lot of the concepts in *Getting to Yes*, as well as the BATNA techniques we covered above. A quick online search will point you in the direction of a wealth of negotiation advice—use your journalistic and research savvy to determine what might be of use to you.

You can also look to freelance unions and collectives for help, as many of them provide contract and negotiation support to their members. You can find more information on these groups in the next chapter.

Omar Mouallem

nonfiction writer and filmmaker

O mar Mouallem was still in film school in Vancouver when he pitched his first story.

"There was a rapper I really liked named Brother Ali. I wanted to talk to him and needed a reason. And I went to school with a music journalist, so I was like, 'Well, he does this and he gets to talk to these really famous musicians that he loves,'" says Mouallem.

So he went to Google to find out how to reach out to the publicist. He secured an interview and it was all going great ... until they asked when and where the story would be published.

"So I scrambled to find one. And I sent two pitches out simultaneously to two different places, which is such a no-no, you would never do that," he says. "The pitch itself was weirdly pandering. I read it aloud recently and was just mortified."

Despite the rocky start, Mouallem found that he loved writing and interviewing, and began to pursue it over film work. He started pitching more stories—arts stories, music and film reviews, and artist interviews. It took about six or seven months before he was paid for his stories, starting at 10 cents a word. Three years later, he started interning at Avenue Magazine in Edmonton.

Photo credit: Aaron Pedersen

What started as an internship turned into an assistant editor job. Then associate editor.

For Mouallem, it was the perfect training ground for freelance work.

"I just learned how to be a freelancer by working with freelancers. I learned how to pitch, I learned how to be a professional," he says. "And I learned what not to be, from experiences that had gone sour."

It also helped him understand the business of magazine writing.

"An editorial internship, if you can land one, is so valuable to see what professionals are doing to fact-check their work, handle their contracts, that kind of stuff. I learned how to invoice. I learned how to negotiate a contract. I learned what the value of your work is, who pays what and how much you should expect to get paid."

After about four and a half years at Avenue, Mouallem wanted to focus on writing rather than editing. He decided to make the move to full-time freelance.

"I told myself that if I can make $35,000 a year, I will do this a second year. And if I don't, then I'm not cut out for it and I need to go back and try to find a staff position somewhere," he says. "But it worked out. I mean, I made double that in my first year."

Early on, Mouallem developed a methodical hustle to his work. He scheduled Fridays to develop and send out pitches, usually two new ones every week.

"I was very realistic about where I would pitch them," he explains. "I knew that I wanted to write for national and eventually international magazines, but I wasn't in a hurry. I thought it was more important for me to get really good at writing for regional magazines, which pay a comparable rate."

Mouallem says it took two to three years for everything to start to come together. By working consistently and strategically, he worked his way up to stories in Wired, Rolling Stone, NewYorker.com, and The Guardian. While he reveled in seeing his work in glossy print, it was about more than the clipping.

"I knew that, from then on, Wired will be in my bio—but, maybe more importantly—from then on, I can feel comfortable pitching any Condé Nast publication."

When negotiating contracts, Mouallem believes it's important to know what rights you hold, and what you're giving away. And he always pushes to maintain his copyright.

"Typically, with the publications I've worked for, there has been a non-exclusive copyright, where they have rights to the copy for [a] set period of time," he says. "It's usually until one year after publication, sometimes it's until the next issue, whether that be three months or one month."

As Mouallem explains, there are many reasons to keep the copyright on what you write.

"It's important because articles become books, articles sometimes do get resold to other places. I've resold stories to Reader's Digest four or five times," he says.

And if you're pitching a piece that's part of a bigger story, this is the kind of work that can lead to bigger projects—if you have the rights.

"Once I turned an article into a documentary. I saw the potential for stories of a certain length and weight to also be bigger film projects ... It's the big stories that could become documentaries, films, and podcasts."

Chapter 9:

Freelance work in the bigger picture

In this chapter ...

- Where is journalism headed?
- The bigger-picture challenges of working free-lance and what's causing them
- Understanding your rights as a worker, and how you can help enforce them

As you've made your way through this book (or picked and scanned the most interesting chapters!) you've likely started to notice that working as a freelance journalist is full of contradictions. It's an industry we often hear is dying, yet more people are consuming media than ever. On one hand, you're told you work for yourself—but are limited by which places take your pitches and publish your work. And while you're technically an office of one, you're part of a fast-growing group of workers across North America: gig workers.

You've likely read a lot about the gig economy—and it ranges from marveling at how it's revolutionizing the world of work to how it's a sign of the failure of capitalism. But, as a journalist, you know that context is key, and that acknowledging and understanding systems—whether it's how City Council passes by-laws or how colleges and universities are funded—helps us see the story in the big picture. That's what this chapter is about: looking at freelance work in the greater labor context so you can better see your place within it and make decisions that work for you.

Is journalism dying?

Depending on who you talk to, there can be a lot of doom and gloom about pursuing a career in the media industry. Whether it's a family member at Thanksgiving dinner telling you that newspapers are dead, or the constant hum of social media on how hard it is to break into the industry, it's understandable to feel like the odds are against you.

On the other hand, in 2020, people around the world consumed more than 7.5 hours of media every day—and Americans spent about equal amounts watching, reading, and listening to traditional media as they did digital. By the numbers, journalism certainly isn't dead, or even dying. But if there's one thing we *do* know about the media landscape, it's changing—and at a remarkable pace. As we've seen in the transition to digital media, there are many jobs and opportunities out there, from traditional employment to jobs at start-ups to freelance and contract gigs. You've no doubt read and heard about the start-ups and the Next New Thing.... And, well, some of them are more successful than others. Part of your job is to do your research as you navigate these options and make informed decisions about what you want to be involved with.

You may find that some of your mentors or professors have little to no experience with the new media world—some may be quick to denounce it, others may be supportive but unable to provide advice for your next steps. Or you may find a mentor who's in the thick of it and able to help you in specific and actionable ways, and that's fantastic! Either way, it's important to maintain those relationships and learn what you can—recognizing, of course, that final decisions are always up to you.

Working for yourself—or supporting a company's bottom line?

Any which way you do the math, a freelance hire is cheaper than an employee. Companies need to provide employees with office space, gear, salaries, vacation pay, perhaps benefits or pensions—all things that they don't pay for when they hire you, as a freelancer, to produce a piece.

As a freelancer, you miss out on those long-term benefits, though many freelancers will account for this discrepancy by charging more to cover those losses when they can. It doesn't mean you can't make a good living as a freelancer, but the odds aren't stacked in your favor that you will. This all takes place in the context of shrinking newsrooms and fewer full-time journalism jobs ... which begs the question: as freelancers, are we contributing to work environments that won't pay journalists properly for their work?

By the numbers, it's evident that newsrooms are using freelancers as a cheaper alternative to fill gaps in their staffing. But does that mean you hold out on principle and don't work freelance? Probably not. After all, freelancing is a way to support yourself using your skills in a work world where permanent full-time jobs are decreasing across the board, not just in journalism.

And then there's the other side of it—with the stability of a permanent, full-time position harder to find, many freelancers say that working for themselves and maintaining a diverse clientele actually gives them *more* job security. By not depending on a single job that could be gone in the next wave of media cuts, their work is flexible and they can ride the ebb and flow of changes in the mediasphere. After all, losing one client when you have 10 or more is less of a hit than losing your only employer who pays your entire salary.

Is freelance causing the demise of the traditional newsroom, or is freelance the outcome of a shattered media landscape where even the well-intentioned outlets are trying to figure out how to cover costs in an online world? Does working freelance for these companies further encourage them to shed full-time jobs? Perhaps, or perhaps those jobs were going to go anyway.

On the other hand, freelance opportunities can help you build your resume and even lead to a coveted permanent spot in a newsroom, if that's your goal. Because of the power imbalance between these outlets and yourself as an individual, it means you will need to decide and enforce what work terms are acceptable to you. Do you take a low-paying contract that you know is undercutting your worth, because you also know that you need to make rent this month? It might help you out of a jam, but it also may set you up to take that lower rate down the line, or encourage the company to keep underpaying. Ultimately, there are no right or wrong answers in these cases, and you need to make decisions that are right for you—even if that means passing on a job.

Living your dreams vs. making a paycheck

Online, you probably see a lot of people promoting entrepreneurship and hustle culture as a way to live life on your own terms: work where you want, when you want, doing what you want. And the truth is, that rationale only really works if money isn't a priority.

Part of the appeal for someone to hire a freelancer is that you're flexible—and that you meet their deadlines. You of course get to agree to the terms, but there isn't always much negotiating room ... and turning down projects means turning down money. Just like negotiating a contract with a major outlet, there's that power imbalance that you have to navigate—and as you may have guessed, you're usually not the big fish!

So, while your schedule is technically yours to decide, the projects you take on will dictate your schedule—and that can include a lot of late nights, weekends, and waiting on sources and interviews. This also applies to the type of work you take on—many tout freelancing as a way to pitch and produce passion projects, but there are times where a paycheck may be what influences you to take on a project. You will likely find yourself balancing work that pays well with the work you truly love doing.

Ultimately, you can always say no to work—but it will likely be a long while before you feel settled enough in your freelance career that you can comfortably turn down work that isn't a good fit or doesn't work with your schedule.

And then, there's the hustle.

Is freelance forever?

Freelancing, particularly full-time freelancing, is constant—being responsible for it means it will likely be on your mind 24/7. For some, this is thrilling, and for others it's a burden. Some people thrive on selling themselves, pitching ideas, balancing multiple projects and running their own business—and for others, it's a means to an end. Whether you love the hustle or not, sustainability and burnout were the two most common topics that came up when I spoke with freelancers about their work.

At the outset of your career, freelancing is a fantastic opportunity to try out new things. It's the full-spread buffet for working in media. You get to work in varying formats, be published with different outlets, learn from new editors, and build your resume. If you want to try a new beat or learn a new skill—pitch it and dive in! Freelancing can help you find your footing in the media world through experience and can also be a stepping stone to a full-time job.

On the other hand, many freelancers I've spoken to see the business side as the necessary evil to doing what they love, especially when full-time jobs aren't available. And, as they grow in their skills, they have a hard time figuring out how to move forward in a job that doesn't exactly have promotions or natural next steps. As they get older, they value the options for parental leave, for health insurance, for a pension—and may move into a job that offers those benefits.

One comment that I heard from many freelancers is that **you aren't a failure if you decide to quit freelance work**. Being honest with yourself, and pursuing a working situation where you are happy and healthy, is so much more important than hacking things out in a place where you are stressed or struggling.

Freelance work can take many forms, from a full-time business to a side business you supplement with more steady work; it might even be a time that helps you make it through the gap between permanent, full-time jobs. Freelance doesn't have to be permanent, and it's OK to let it go when it isn't working for you. Once you gain some experience and better understand the realities of freelancing, it will start to become easier for you to tell when it's worth the time and effort, and when it isn't.

Systemic problems, collective solutions

While you might see yourself as embarking on your own as a freelancer, you're still part of a collective; in fact, you're part of one of the fastest-growing sectors of employment across North America: gig work. In the United States, 59 million people worked freelance in some way, shape, or form in 2020. The latest data from Statistics Canada shows that more than 1.7 million people did gig work in 2016, and that number has very likely grown since.

The world of freelance is often a lonely one, where you're seen as working by yourself for yourself. And while this is true, it ignores the realities of the social, cultural, and capital systems you work in as a freelancer. In her book, *Writers' Rights: Freelance Journalism in a Digital Age* (2016), Nicole Cohen talks about how individualism and independence are seen as hallmarks of freelance work—but it's this isolation that can work against them.

"Journalism is very byline driven. It's about the individual writer. So that comes with a whole bunch of ideas around individual creative artists rather than thinking of yourself as a worker, or part of a bigger production process," says Cohen, who is an associate professor at the Institute of Communication, Culture, Information, and Technology at the University of Toronto Mississauga.

"A lot of it has something to do with neo-liberalism—the era we've been in for 40 years pushes an ideology of individualism, of meritocracy, of competitive individualism rather than solidarity and care and connection ... A capitalist economy encourages people to be individually concerned about themselves. Competing with one another for scarce jobs [and] resources like this, historically, tends to drive people apart rather than bring us all together."

One of the biggest dangers that comes with an individualist mindset as a freelancer is the assumption that you have control over everything—and that if you're having problems working as a freelancer, it's up to you to solve them. Not making enough money? Just take on more jobs, regardless of the stress it puts on you. Having problematic conversations with an editor? Play nice, or find somewhere else to sell your work. While these may be short-term solutions, they ultimately ignore the colonial, racist, and capitalist systems that most newsrooms and the media as an industry work within. These are systems that benefit from keeping things the way they are, systems that require collective action and legislation to change.

Historically, collective action through unions is where workers have been able to negotiate better working conditions. Limited work hours, employment insurance, health and disability benefits, pensions, guaranteed hours or job stability, diversity and equity initiatives—these are all realities because workers used their leverage as a group to negotiate with their employer.

While unions might seem like a thing of the past, there has been a recent increase in newsrooms that have organized. In 2015, VICE's workers unionized, and were followed by Gizmodo, the Guardian US, Salon.com, and the Huffington Post. VICE Canada followed in 2016, with their employees ratifying their first collective agreement a year later.

In fact, more than 100 outlets across the US have organized since 2015, and a half a dozen in Canada. That's the focus of Cohen's current research.

"When I wrote my book [*Writers' Rights*], it was very hard for the freelancers that I interviewed and surveyed and talked to to identify as workers. There was a real lack of a labor consciousness," she says. "[In] 10 years, there's been a massive shift in that. I would call it a class consciousness around media work and journalism and freelancing, where people realize they're workers and they may love the work they do and the job they do, but they are getting exploited in a technical sense by media companies."

Cohen credits many factors for the shift, including the Occupy Wall Street protests, Bernie Sanders's presidential nomination run, increasing visibility of the Black Lives Matter movement, and renewed feminist activism—all inherently connected to issues of equity, equality, and labor.

"I think Millennials and Gen Z have realized what precarious work means and that they're not immune to it, especially in media," says Cohen. "There's been a real uptick in organizing—solidarity organizing. So not necessarily even unionizing to negotiate better freelance rates, but kind of just coming together to say that we are better and stronger as a collective force."

This benefits freelancers in two main ways: first, some of these unions are including rights for freelancers in their collective agreements. Second, there has been an increase in freelancers organizing in non-traditional unions to negotiate benefits for gig workers.

One example is the Freelancers Union, based in Brooklyn and comprised of more than 500,000 members across the United States. Since the union organized in 1995, it has been a resource for freelancers and an advocate around freelance issues, but it has also used the size of its membership to help negotiate and offer freelancer-oriented health, life, and work-related insurance benefits for its members. In 2016, they were also at the front of a campaign in New York City to enact the Freelance Isn't Free law, which helps protect freelancers from clients who don't pay. During the COVID-19 pandemic, the Freelancers Union also pushed to include freelance workers in the national relief packages.

"I think that has really highlighted the need for some of these traditional employee programs to be extended to the independent worker," says Rafael Espinal, the union's president and executive director. "I think those conversations are also going to start proliferating as we move forward."

It's all a big misclassification

Another issue within freelance work is job classification—or rather, job *mis*classification. For many freelance jobs, the work can look a lot like employment ... without the benefits. Some states have introduced legislation to help address this.

"The intention of those bills is to create the distinction between a traditional employee and independent worker because I think we all know that, in a lot of industries, employers would hire a freelancer to do full-time work and treat them as if they were a traditional employee without giving them the protections that come with being an employee," says Espinal.

This is particularly important as the majority of freelancers are women and racialized workers—it's a matter of equity that these workers are afforded these rights if they are in fact working as employees. But the language of the legislation has had unintended consequences, like discouraging companies from hiring independent workers. States like California have already begun revising their laws to better serve the bill's intentions, and the Freelancers Union hopes to help with the upcoming reforms.

Another side of misclassification is understanding what your work as a freelancer is—while many may equate freelance journalism with entrepreneurial journalism, the two concepts are very different. Entrepreneurial journalism is starting your own media outlet—like Jeremy Klaszus, founder of The Sprawl, who you met in chapter 3. It's building a company or business, and follows more of the culture of being an entrepreneur or traditional business owner. As a freelance journalist, you're a team of one—a self-employed worker. Neither is better or worse than the other, but understanding your work situation and goals will make it easier to make decisions as you navigate your career. After all, what works for a media start-up probably won't work for a solo journalist.

Creating your own collective

By working alone, freelancers miss out on the ability to bargain collectively—you negotiate each and every one of your contracts independently. But you can still use the concepts behind collective action to help inform your work as a freelancer, and to improve your working conditions. For example, think of when you negotiate contracts and fees—by working alone, you may not have an idea of what's a fair wage, or what an outlet has paid others before. By talking to other freelancers and using online resources, you can get a better picture of what others are being paid and how you should price your work.

You can't join a traditional union as a freelancer, but there's an increasing number of unions and organizations that support freelancers, from the Freelancers Union in the United States to the Canadian Freelance Guild, the Canadian Freelance Union, or the CWA Canada Associate Members program. Some of these groups have fees, others don't, and they serve as a place to connect with other freelancers, develop skills, and learn more about the industry. Membership can also give you access to discounts for insurance, benefits, or other services you might use in your freelance work.

Beyond the more formalized union environment, there are many ways to connect with others, from starting your own group chat with your freelancer friends to joining existing message boards, Slack groups, and more. Talking to other freelancers will be a big help as you start out and are learning—so use the power of the hive mind to your advantage. It can be difficult to break out of the hyper-competitiveness that the journalism industry can promote, but by sharing information, like rates of pay and contracts, you will be able to improve your freelance opportunities as well as others'. Seek out mentors where you can, and be that mentor to someone else when you have the opportunity. There are a lot of issues, economic and social, that you will navigate in the world of freelance—and having friends and colleagues to support you won't just make it easier, but more enjoyable, too.

Desmond Cole

independent journalist, activist, and author

Desmond Cole never had plans to become a journalist, but he always loved to write.

"I was always a writer, but I was a writer for myself. I would write in journals and I would write little things and they would always be for me," he says. "So I started a blog. It really couldn't be said to be journalism. It was my reflections about things—often, things that were upsetting me."

It was years into writing his blog that Torontoist, a local website, asked to republish a piece he wrote against a program that was putting police officers in schools across in the city.

"It was an honor and it was a nice feeling. That was the time that I started wanting to do something like that regularly, where I thought it would be so cool if I could do this on a regular basis for Torontoist or for somebody else," he says.

It was the start of his freelance career—sort of.

"Torontoist told me upfront, very clearly, that they had no money. So a freelancer, like myself, when I submitted a piece to Torontoist, I was paid $15."

For $15 an article, Cole wasn't about to quit his day job. But that same year, 2010, Toronto elected a new mayor—Rob Ford.

Photo credit: Kate Yang-Nikodym

Previously a conservative city councilor, he would gain international notoriety for recording a video making death threats, admitting to using crack cocaine, using inappropriate language in front of the media, and more.

"A lot of people were afraid of Rob Ford. I was afraid of Rob Ford. And when Rob Ford won, covering his city hall became very important for once."

Cole began reporting on committee meetings, town halls, and other local events—and discovered that he loved the work and thrived on telling stories in his community from his perspective as a Black journalist. Thanks to other freelancers and colleagues, he learned how to shoot video, take photos, and edit his multimedia work. His work with Torontoist gained traction in local media circles. Through all of this, he continued to keep a non-reporting job, whether it was working as an office manager or serving at a café.

When Michael Brown was shot and killed by police in Ferguson, Missouri, in August 2014, Cole knew he had to go and report on the protests himself. By November, he was able to work with The Walrus magazine to cover his flight and hotel, though they didn't pay for his writing and reporting. Cole fundraised for his other expenses, from meals to safety equipment to batteries for his gear. He landed the day after the jury voted not to indict Darren Wilson, the officer who shot Brown.

"I didn't get paid a dime. And I was so happy to be there," Cole says. "I wanted to do this work and it wasn't about money."

As one of the only Canadian reporters in Ferguson at the time, other major Canadian news outlets asked Cole to do live hits from the field. They didn't offer any compensation, and Cole was too excited about the opportunity to ask about payment.

One of Cole's best-known pieces of reporting came out the next year—a cover story for Toronto Life magazine where he shared his first-person account with carding and the Toronto Police Service. Years of research has shown that the practice is disproportionately aimed at Black men. The piece, which won three National Magazine Awards, was one of Toronto Life's most-read articles and led Cole to new reporting opportunities, including a gig as a columnist for the Toronto Star.

Cole resigned from his column at the Star in 2017, after being accused of violating journalistic policies for protesting a Toronto Police Services Board meeting about the service's practice of carding and racial profiling. Many disagreed publicly with the Star's decision, noting other columnists for the paper who regularly engage in activism. It was this experience that led to Cole's first book, *The Skin We're In: A Year of Black Resistance and Power*, that came out in 2020 and quickly became a national bestseller.

Though he would have loved to work in a major newsroom, Cole says it never would have allowed him to do the reporting he wants to do.

"Being a freelance journalist and making your way is increasingly difficult, and if you don't conform to these ideas of objectivity and neutrality, which just reinforce power and the status quo, and it's really hard to get anywhere," he says. "Black and Indigenous and other racialized journalists, women, queer and trans people in the newsroom, disabled people in the newsroom, where are the places for us to have our lived experience, to make a difference in how we record the news?"

As he promotes his book and continues his activism work, including speaking publicly on issues of race and racism, Cole still sees journalism as the heart of what he does.

"I think of journalism now as a practice more than a career—a set of thoughts and a way of thinking about the world, a way of analyzing, approaching storytelling," says Cole. "And what's fascinating is the next generation of journalists who are going to take the industry in completely new directions, exciting ones."

Last thoughts

And so, we've made it to the end. We've looked at the creative side of freelance journalism: how to develop your brand and build your network, and how to research, craft, and submit your pitches. We've also looked at the business side of freelance: how to imagine your business, organize your finances, invoice and plan for taxes, and how to negotiate contracts and the law.

As you've no doubt figured out by this point, freelancing is a balancing act—moving between the tension of its creative and business elements, all while juggling multiple pitches, projects, and people. It can lead to some of the most interesting and fulfilling projects you will ever work on ... and it can also be a lot of effort and a lot of stress. Freelance certainly isn't for everyone—and whether you're now ready to break out and try it for yourself, or whether you have no interest whatsoever, you're making the right choice for you.

I hope you have found a lesson or two in this book that will be helpful as you set off on your career. The great thing about understanding freelancing is that you can apply these concepts to all facets of your life, whether it's using informational interview skills to prepare for a job interview or planning your personal finances and filing your taxes. But please, don't take this guide as the end all, be all for freelancing—consider it a jumping-off point and feel free to tweak, shift, or change things altogether if and when they don't work for you. Freelance has never been a one-size-fits-all situation, and with the constant change in the media landscape, you will encounter so many unique scenarios that you will get to navigate in your own way.

When those scenarios do arise—do your research, trust your gut, and try your best. And, when you inevitably make a mistake along the way, don't beat yourself up too much ... it's those lessons that will help you grow to be an even better journalist (and, I daresay, a better person).

All the best in your next steps.

Index

Note: Page numbers in *italics* denote figures.

From the Publisher

A name never says it all, but the word "Broadview" expresses a good deal of the philosophy behind our company. We are open to a broad range of academic approaches and political viewpoints. We pay attention to the broad impact book publishing and book printing has in the wider world; for some years now we have used 100% recycled paper for most titles. Our publishing program is internationally oriented and broad-ranging. Our individual titles often appeal to a broad readership too; many are of interest as much to general readers as to academics and students.

Founded in 1985, Broadview remains a fully independent company owned by its shareholders—not an imprint or subsidiary of a larger multinational.

To order our books or obtain up-to-date information, please visit broadviewpress.com.

broadview press
www.broadviewpress.com